W9-BIH-675

MASSEY TRACTOR

DATA BOOK

Keith D. Oltrogge

MBI Publishing Company

First published in 1999 by MBI Publishing Company, PO Box 1,
729 Prospect Avenue, Osceola, WI 54020-0001 USA

MBI Publishing Company books are also available at discounts in bulk quantity
for industrial or sales-promotional use. For details write to Special Sales Manager
at Motorbooks International Wholesalers & Distributors, 729 Prospect Avenue,
PO Box 1, Osceola, WI 54020-0001 USA.

Library of Congress Cataloging-in-Publication Data Available
ISBN 0-7603-0599-4

On the front cover: In 1939, Massey-Harris added the name "Super" to
distinguish it from the 101 Model with the beefy 201-cubic-inch engine from
the 101 Junior that boasted only 124 cubic inches. At the time, the 101 Super
Row Crop was the most stylish and advanced in the line. The streamlined
sheet metal completely enclosed the engine—nearly unheard of in the tractor
industry at that time. Today, the Super 101s with vented side panels, like the
model on the cover, are among the most collected Massey-Harris Tractors.
Randy Leffingwell

On the back cover: Between 1946 and 1955, the Model 44 and its derivatives
were clearly the most popular tractors in the Massey-Harris line. With
production peaking at nearly 25,000 in 1951, the Model 44 accounted for half
of the company's tractor sales in 1950-1951. The factory press release photo
pictures a now-rare 44 Special LP tractor equipped with the 260-cubic-inch
engine, the first LP tractor offered by Massey-Harris.

Printed in the United States of America

Contents

Introduction

This book recaps the tractors sold by Massey-Harris and its predecessor company, Wallis Tractor Company. Massey-Harris evolved as a world leader in manufacturing farm machinery from an 1891 merger of the Massey Company, founded by Daniel Massey in 1847, and the A. Harris Company, founded by Alanson Harris in 1857.

Massey-Harris entered into tractor sales in 1917 by forming an agreement with the Bull Tractor Company of Minneapolis to sell the Big Bull tractors through Massey-Harris dealers in Canada. The Big Bull apparently never carried the Massey-Harris name. The Big Bull tractor proved to have a poor design, and in 1918, Massey-Harris entered into an agreement to build and sell the Parrett Tractor in Canada under the Massey-Harris name. These tractors were built at Weston, Ontario, with parts designed by the Parrett Tractor Company of Chicago and cast at the Massey-Harris plants in Canada. The Parrett-designed tractor remained in production until 1922, when engineering support for the outdated design from the troubled Parrett Company started to disintegrate.

In 1926, Massey-Harris entered into an agreement with the J.I. Case Plow Works to sell Wallis tractors through Massey-Harris dealers in the United States and Canada. The origin of the Wallis tractor traces back to 1902, when Robert O. Hendrickson began designing the Bear tractor. Hendrickson tested the designs until 1911, when the J.I. Case Plow Works purchased the Wallis Tractor Company. The following year, Case began selling the Bear and the Cub Wallis tractors.

The J.I. Case Plow Works of Racine, Wisconsin, was a separate company from the J.I. Case Threshing Machine Company, also of Racine. The J.I. Case Plow Works was run by Henry Wallis, a son-in-law of J.I. Case. In 1928, the Massey-Harris Company purchased the J.I. Case Plow Works for $2.4 million, then sold the exclusive rights for the J.I. Case name back to the J.I. Case Threshing Machine Company for $700,000. Massey-Harris now had a well-designed tractor, an established engineering staff, a tractor factory, and a network of U.S. dealers. It had established its presence in the United States as a major tractor manufacturer.

The Wallis tractor was a very well-designed machine. Engineering firsts for the original Wallis design and its successive models included:
1. Being the first tractor company to use a four-cylinder tractor motor,

2. Being first to use a steel U-frame integrating the engine and frame for lighter weight and greater strength,
3. Being the first tractor to use removable cylinder sleeves,
4. Being the first tractor to deliver motor power to the drawbar through a live rear axle,
5. Being the first to use an oil-bath air cleaner, and
6. Being first to use removable valve inserts.

In spite of resounding success, the Wallis name was phased out, and by 1932, all tractors built in Racine had the Massey-Harris name.

The Racine plant continued to build tractors until 1958, when all tractor manufacturing was transferred to the Ferguson plant in Detroit. Massey brought the Ferguson tractor into the family through a merger of the Massey-Harris Company and the Harry Ferguson Company in 1953. Both companies continued to build and sell their own tractors through their own dealer networks until 1958, when they were brought together to form the Massey-Ferguson Company.

This book provides details on all Massey-Harris and Wallis tractors sold through Massey dealers from 1912 through 1957, including serial numbers, specifications, and production data. Tractors built after 1957 bear the Massey-Ferguson name and were descendants of the Ferguson tractor.

Tractor model variations such as axle or sheet metal type (standard, Row-Crop, orchard, vineyard, highcrop) and engine fuel variations (gas, LP, diesel, distillate) are covered under the basic model section for tractor model. Unfortunately, Massey-Harris archival information is not very detailed or complete regarding production information on some models of tractors, especially the pre–World War II models. The company didn't retain post–World War II production information for axle and engine variations on most models. Thus, it is not possible to determine how many model 44 diesel tractors were built out of the total model 44 production.

Most information contained herein is based on original sales catalogs, parts books, and owner's manuals. Personal insight has been added based on the author's own knowledge, acquired through years of discussions with other collectors and former Massey employees.

Big Bull

The Big Bull tractor was built in Minneapolis by the Bull Tractor Company. An agreement was made in 1916 with Massey-Harris in Canada for the Massey-Harris dealers to be exclusive distributors of the Big Bull tractor in Canada. The Massey dealers in Canada marketed the Big Bull from late 1916 through 1917. The tractor proved to be unreliable and had many problems. By the end of 1917, Massey-Harris discontinued Big Bull tractor sales.

Production Figures: Unavailable

Serial Numbers: Unavailable

Tractor: Length: 163 inches; width: 78 inches; height overall: 78 inches; weight: 4,870 pounds; speed: 2.41 miles per hour; operator's seat on platform, rear end; all levers, carburetor, magneto control, and oiling system within easy reach of operator.

Power: 12 horsepower on drawbar; 24 horsepower on belt.

Painted: Aluminum.

Drive Wheel: 14-inch face; 1/2x1 1/2-inch forged head spokes; hot riveted top and bottom; equipped with Hyatt high-duty roller bearings.

Traction Lugs: 32 4 1/2-inch subsoiling spade lugs; 24 cone lugs for road work (above is regular equipment); 16 angle bar cross cleats (spade lugs or cross cleats were optional when purchaser specified with order).

Land Wheel: 40 inches high; 8 inches wide; roller bearings.

Land Wheel Drive: Clutch on counter shaft to high-grade roller links chain to sprocket; roller pinion and internal sprocket attached to Land Wheel.

Front Wheel: 30 inches high; 6 inches wide; 3-inch center rib; bearing, removal bushing.

Steering Gear: Worm gear and sector.

Transmission: Direct through spur gear and roller pinion to Bull Wheel; drive pinion, drop forged, machine cut teeth, hardened; spur gear, semi-steel; roller pinion, nine rollers and pins, each one separate; steel hardened; lubricated by grease through pin to inside of roller, on outside by drip oiler.

Clutch: External contracting around flange on fly wheel; no end thrust on crankshaft bearing; no wood blocks to adjust; Thermoid lining; arm passes over center to hold it in position; no strain on retaining collar; single adjusting nut.

Belt Pulley: 6 1/2-inch face; 12-inch diameter.

Big Bull Tractor.

Motor: Two-cylinder opposed L-head; 5 1/2-inch bore; 7-inch stroke; four-cycle; governor controlled; speed 750 rpm.

Governor: Fly ball enclosed in motor; direct connected and full control of butterfly valve; lubricated from overflow from oil distributing box; hand throttle control.

Fuel: Kerosene; gasoline; distillate.

Tanks: Kerosene: 18 1/2 gallons, electrically welded; gasoline: 3 1/2 gallons, electrically welded; drip oiler: 2 gallons, soldered.

Cooling: Copper tube radiator, forced circulation by centrifugal circulating water pump; large fan, belt driven.

Oiling System: Forced circulation, oil used over and over; plunger pump operated from camshaft; lifts oil from main reservoir to distributing box. Is a positive force feed; in full view of operator.

Ignition: High tension impulse starter magneto, standard make (no batteries).

Carburetor: Standard make fitted with kerosene vaporizer; kerosene or gasoline burner, can be switched at will of operator.

Sawyer-Massey Tractors

The Massey family owned a 40 percent interest in the Sawyer-Massey Company. This company had no corporate relationship with the Massey-Harris Company other than the two companies cooperating in the marketing of threshing machines. The Massey family withdrew its interest in the Sawyer-Massey Company in 1910. The Massey name, however, was retained and appeared on five tractors in the 1910–1921 period.

Production Figures: Unavailable
Serial Numbers: Unavailable

Model 10-20
Motor: Four-cylinder, 4 1/4x4 3/4-inch stroke, Waukesha built.
Ignition: Magneto.
Lubrication: Force feed.
Speeds: Two forward, one reverse. 2 1/4 and 3 1/2 miles per hour.
Belt Pulley: 21-inch diameter, 8-inch face.
Wheels: Front: 28x5-inch face; rear: 54x14-inch face.
Length/Width: 133 inches/61 inches.
Weight: 5,200 pounds.
Rating: 10 horsepower drawbar; 20 horsepower belt.

Model 11-22
Motor: Four-cylinder, 4x6-inch stroke, Erd built.
Ignition: Magneto.
Lubrication: Force feed.
Speeds: Two forward, one reverse. 2 1/4 and 3 1/2 miles per hour.
Belt Pulley: 21-inch diameter, 8-inch face.
Wheels: Front: 28x5-inch face; rear: 54x14-inch face.
Length/Width: 133 inches/61 inches.
Weight: 5,200 pounds.
Rating: 11 horsepower drawbar; 22 horsepower belt.

Model 16-32
Motor: Four-cylinder, 5x7 1/2-inch stroke.
Ignition: Magneto.
Lubrication: Force feed.
Speeds: Two forward, one reverse. 2 1/4 and 3 1/2 miles per hour.
Belt Pulley: 27-inch diameter, 9-inch face.
Wheels: Front: 38x8 inches; rear: 62x20 inches.
Length/Width: 173 inches/81 inches.
Rating: 16 horsepower drawbar; 32 horsepower belt.

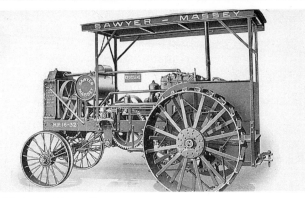

16-32 Sawyer-Massey Tractor.

Model 20-40

Motor: Four-cylinder, 680 rpm, 5.625x7-inch stroke.
Carburetor: 2-inch Kingston.
Ignition: High tension magneto with impulse starter.
Lubrication: Force feed and splash.
Speeds: Two forward and two reverse. 2 and 3 miles per hour.
Belt Pulley: 27-inch diameter and 8-inch face, 340 rpm.
Wheels: Front: 38x8 inches; rear: 62x20 inches.
Length/Width: 173 inches/81 inches.
Weight: 11,800 pounds.
Rating: 4-6 plow; 20 horsepower drawbar; 40 horsepower belt.

Model 25-45 (re-rated 27-50 in 1917)

Motor: Four-cylinder, 600 rpm, 6.25x8-inch stroke.
Carburetor: 2-inch Kingston.
Ignition: High tension magneto.
Lubrication: Force feed and splash.
Speeds: Two forward and two reverse. 2 and 3 1/2 miles per hour.
Belt Pulley: 32-inch diameter and 10-inch face, 300 rpm.
Wheels: Front: 40x12-inch; rear: 68x30-inch.
Length/Width: 190 inches/108 inches.
Weight: 17,500 pounds.
Rating: 6-8 plow; 25 horsepower drawbar; 50 horsepower belt.

Massey-Harris Number 1 and Number 2

In 1918, Massey-Harris entered into an agreement with the Parrett Tractor Company of Chicago, Illinois, to manufacture a tractor based on Parrett patents and design in Massey's Toronto factory. In 1919, production was moved to Weston, Ontario. The Massey Number 1 was identical to the Parrett tractor. Massey's agreement with Parrett allowed Massey dealers in Canada, Australia, New Zealand, and the United Kingdom to sell these tractors. The Number 2 is almost identical to the Number 1, except the Number 2 has shields and covers on the tractor's bull pinions and drive gears, and had a belt guide mounted directly in front of the belt pulley.

Production Figures:	1918–1919	125
	1920	382
	1921	39
	Total	546

Serial Numbers: Unavailable.

Dimensions: Total length: 12 feet. Width: 6 feet. Height: 5 feet, 6 inches. Wheelbase: 92 inches.

Wheels: Rear 60-inch diameter, 10-inch face. Choice of five kinds of lugs. Front 46-inch diameter, 4-inch face with high center rib.

Frame: 7 inch steel channel with substantial steel angle cross bars and braces.

Motor: Four-cylinder, four-cycle vertical, 4 1/4x5 1/2 inches with self-contained positive oiling system; high tension Kingston magneto with impulse starter; runs on gasoline or kerosene. Built by Buda (Model HTU).

Carburetor: Kingston Model LD 1 1/4 inches.

Rating: 12 horsepower on the drawbar, 3,000 pounds pull; 22 horsepower on the brake at 1,000 rpm.

Clutch: three-plate, enclosed, and running in oil.

Transmission: Spur gear drive on high and low gear. Self-aligning ball bearings and roller bearings; gears and bearings run in oil.

Speeds: Forward, low, 1 3/4 miles per hour. Forward, high, 2 3/8 miles per hour. Reverse 1.8 miles per hour.

Belt Pulley: 12 inches in diameter, 7-inch leather face, mounted directly on extension of engine shaft running at 1,000 rpm, giving a belt speed of 3,142 feet per minute.

Cooling System: Capacity, 7 gallons; radiator has exceptionally large cooling surface, honeycomb-type of an improved pattern.

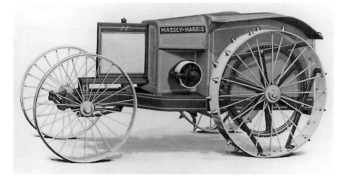

Massey-Harris Model No. 1 Tractor.

Governor: Built-in type, operating on the throttle; effective and economical on fuel.

Capacity of Tanks: Kerosene: 16 gallons; gasoline: 2 gallons; water: 3 gallons.

Drawbar: 19 inches from ground, pivoted ahead of rear axle.

Weight: 5,200 pounds.

Brake: An effective foot brake operating on a drum on the double gear.

Retail Price: (1922) $1,200

Massey-Harris Model Number 3

In 1921, the No. 2 Massey-Harris tractor was redesigned. The radiator was mounted in the conventional transverse fashion. Only three of these tractors are known to exist today.

Production Figures: 1922   25
                             1923   1
                             Total   26

Serial Numbers: Unavailable

Dimensions: Total length: 12 feet, 9 inches. Width: 6 feet, 6 inches. Height: 5 feet, 6 inches. Wheelbase: 92 inches.

Motor: Four-cylinder, four-cycle vertical Buda engine. 4 1/2x6 1/4 inches.

Rating: 15 horsepower on drawbar; 28 horsepower on belt at 1,000 rpm.

Speeds: Forward, low, 2 1/2 miles per hour; forward, high, 3 1/4 miles per hour; reverse 1.8 miles per hour.

Belt Pulley: 12-inch diameter, 8-inch width.

Weight: 5,800 pounds.

Retail Price: (1924) $1,400

Massey-Harris Model No. 3 Tractor.

Wallis Bear

The Massey-Harris Company purchased in 1928 the J.I. Case Plow Works, which manufactured the Wallis tractor. The line of tractors and tillage equipment was retained by Massey-Harris and the J.I. Case name was sold back to the J.I. Case Threshing Machine Company. The first Wallis tractor was the Wallis Bear. It was also advertised as the "Fuel Save Tractor," Model B, or Model 4-30. Only one Bear tractor is known to exist in the United States today.

Production Figures: 1912–1913: 10
Serial Numbers: 1912–1913: 201–210
Capacity: Average 8 breaker and 10 stubble bottoms.
Drawbar Horsepower: 30.
Belt Horsepower: 50.
Horses Displaced: 30 to 40.
Motor: Four-cylinder, 7 1/2 -inch bore by 8-inch stroke.
Diameter of Crankshaft: 3 inches chrome steel.
Length of Crankshaft Bearings: 32 inches.
Number of Crankshaft Bearings: 5.
Diameter of Drive Wheels: 7 feet.
Width of Drive Wheels: 30 inches.
Diameter of Front Wheel: 42 inches.
Width of Front Wheel: 24 inches.
Total Width: Outside of driver, 92 inches.
Length of Wheelbase: 12 feet.

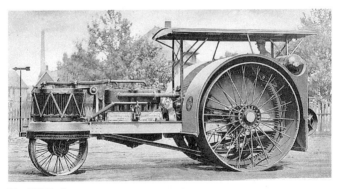

The Wallis Bear.

Diameter of Belt Pulley: 24 inches.

Width of Belt Pulley: 12 inches.

Capacity of Fuel Tanks: 60 gallons.

Radiator Cooling Surface: 8,647.5 square inches, 460 feet of spiral tubing. Oiling: Automatic circulating system.

Transmission: Three-speed sliding gear, selective type.

Speed Range: 1 1/2 to 4 miles per hour.

Steering: Combination power and hand.

Total Weight: 16,000 pounds.

Wallis Cub (Models C and D)

The Wallis Cub was the first Wallis tractor with the U-frame design. The body of the tractor actually served as the oil pan crankcase and transmission housing, eliminating heavy steel girder frames.

Production Figures: 1913–1917: 660

Serial Numbers: 1913–1917: 1001–1660

Capacity: Constant drawbar pull 4,000 pounds. Maximum drawbar pull 5,000 pounds.

Speed: Plowing speed 2 1/4 miles per hour. Road speed 3 1/2 to 4 miles per hour.

Total Weight: 8,500 pounds.

Dimensions: Wheelbase: 102 3/8 inches. Width overall: 6 feet, 2 inches. Height: 7 feet, 3 inches. Length overall: 14 feet, 3 inches.

Motor: Four-cylinder, four-cycle. Cylinders 6-inch diameter 7-inch stroke. Crankshaft 2 3/4-inch diameter with five main bearings, 26 1/4-inch total length. Connecting rods: drop forged. Camshaft: drop forged with cams integral hardened and ground. Valves: special tungsten alloy steel. Governor: hydraulic type. Clutch: three-plate type with copper asbestos friction surfaces.

Cooling System: Enclosed, cellular type. Circulation of water by centrifugal pump driven from front end of crankshaft.

Lubrication: Continuation circulation type. Oil pumped through all motor bearings continually under pressure.

Ignition: K.W. High Tension Magneto with impulse starter. Starts on magneto; no batteries required.

Fuel Tank: Capacity 30 gallons.

Transmission: Two-speed sliding gear, selective type.

Brakes: Individual to each rear wheel. Drums: pressed steel. Bands: steel lined with copper asbestos.

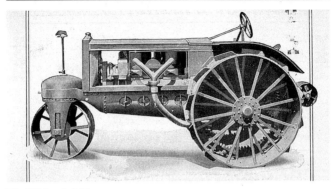

The Wallis Cub Tractor.

Thresher Bracket: Pulley 14-inch diameter, 9-inch face; runs at motor
speed. Control through main motor clutch and independent coupling.

Front Wheel: 14-inch face, 34-inch diameter, suspension type.

Rear Wheel: 20-inch face, 5-inch diameter, suspension type.

Extension Rim: 7 1/2-inch face extensions are furnished as an extra
when ordered.

Springs: Tractor is spring mounted on both front and rear wheels.

Color: Chassis and engine: Wallis gray; wheels: dark red.

Wallis Cub Jr. (Model J)

The Wallis Cub Jr. was a smaller version of the Wallis Cub. It became the basis for most of the Wallis tractors that followed over the next several years.

Production Figures: 1915–1916: 3,505

Serial Numbers: 1915–1916: 10,001–13,505

Drawbar Horsepower: 15.

Belt Horsepower: 25.

Drawbar Pull: 2 1/2 miles per hour; 2,600 pounds maximum; 2,000 pounds constant.

Type of Engine: Vertical four-cylinder, four-cycle, valve-in-head. Cast block, with removable cylinder sleeves.

Bore and Stroke: 4 1/4x5 3/4 inches.

Normal rpm: 850 to 900.

Three Removable Phosphor Bronze Back, Babbitt Lined Main Bearings: Front bearings, 2 1/4-inch diameter by 2 3/4 inches long. Center bearings, 2 1/4-inch diameter by 3 1/4 inches long. Rear bearings, 2 1/4-inch diameter by 4 3/4 inches long.

Weight of Motor: 750 pounds.

Oiling System: Positive pump and splash.

Ignition: K.W., high tension, with impulse starter.

Carburetor: Bennett 1 1/2-inch, gasoline. Kerosene equipment, special.

Governor: Hydraulic type, Wallis make.

Fuel Supply: To carburetor by gravity.

Fuel Tank Capacity: 20 gallons.

The Wallis Cub Jr.

Cooling System: Enclosed, cellular type. Modine "Spirex" radiator.

Water Capacity: 9 gallons.

Water Circulation: By centrifugal pump.

Air Circulation: By belt-driven fan.

Clutch: Expanding shoe type, Wallis make.

Belt Pulley: 18-inch diameter by 6 3/4-inch face, running 430 rpm. Belt pulley located left-hand-side chassis; running forward.

Transmission: Wallis Special, enclosed; two speeds forward.

Drive Wheels: 48-inch diameter by 12-inch face.

Front Wheel: 30-inch diameter by 8-inch face. Mounted on springs and Hyatt roller bearings.

Frame: Wallis patented, boiler plate, "U" shape.

Wheelbase: 100 inches.

Tread: 49 inches.

Total Width: 61 inches, overall.

Total Length: 148 inches, overall.

Turning Radius: Clear outside, 10 feet.

Height of Drawbar: 13 1/2 to 17 inches.

Clearance at Lowest Point: 13 inches.

Total Weight: 3,345 pounds.

Color: Chassis and engine: Wallis gray; wheels: dark red.

Wallis Motor Cultivator

The Wallis Motor Cultivator was built in 1919 as an experimental tractor with a Wisconsin engine. The tractor was actually shown and demonstrated in July 1919 at the Wichita, Kansas, National Tractor Field Demonstrations. Nothing is known about the tractor after this date. None exist today.

Production Figures: Unknown (probably never past experimental production).
Serial Numbers: Unknown.
The J.I. Case Plow Works' two-row motor cultivator weighs 3,160 pounds, is of the three-wheel type, and has a four-cylinder Wisconsin engine, 3 3/4-inch bore by 5-inch stroke, running at 1,200 rpm; Modine radiator; gear drive, runs 2 1/2 and 3 1/2 miles per hour, no pulley, and has 29 inches of ground clearance over corn row.

The Wallis Motor Cultivator.

Wallis Model K and K-3

The tractor is started by using a side crank through the rear wheel into the belt pulley.

Production Figures: 1916–1922: 9,155

Serial Numbers: Model K-3 1916: 14,001–14,441

    Model K 1916–1922: 14,442–23,156

This is the first Wallis tractor tested at the Nebraska Tractor Tests (Test No. 49, August 1920, Serial No. 21166). Drawbar horsepower tested 16.06 horsepower.

Drawbar Horsepower: 15.

Belt Horsepower: 25.

Drawbar Pull: 2 1/2 miles per hour, 2,600 pounds maximum; 2,000 pounds constant.

Wallis Motor: Own make.

Type of Engine: Vertical four-cylinder, four-cycle, valve-in-head. Cast block, with removable cylinder sleeves.

Bore and Stroke: 4 1/4x5 3/4 inches.

Normal rpm: 850 to 900.

Crankshaft: Balanced chrome-vanadium steel, heat-treated. All bearings 2 1/4-inch diameter.

Piston Rings: Three 1/4-inch-wide rings on each piston.

Weight of Motor: 750 pounds.

Oiling System: Positive pump and splash.

Ignition: Berling high tension, with impulse starter. Model EQ41.

Carburetor: Bennett 1 1/4 inch; gasoline, kerosene, distillate. Model H & J.

Governor: Hydraulic type, Wallis make.

Fuel Supply: To carburetor by gravity.

Fuel Tank Capacity: 20 gallons.

Cooling System: Enclosed, cellular type. Modine "Spirex" radiator.

Water Capacity: 6 gallons.

Water Circulation: By centrifugal pump.

Air Circulation: By belt-driven fan.

Clutch: Twin Disc, three-plate type.

Belt Pulley: 18-inch diameter by 6 3/4-inch face, running 430 rpm. Belt pulley located left-hand-side chassis; running forward.

Transmission: Wallis Special, enclosed; two speeds forward, one reverse.

Drive Wheels: 48-inch diameter by 12-inch face.

The Wallis Model K.

Two Front Wheels: 30-inch diameter by 8-inch face. Mounted on
  roller bearings.
Frame: Wallis patented, boiler plate, "U" shape.
Wheelbase: 84 inches.
Tread: 49 inches.
Total Width: 61 inches, overall.
Total Length: 132 inches, overall.
Turning Radius: Clear outside, 10 feet.
Height of Drawbar: 13 1/2 inches to 17 inches.
Clearance at Lowest Point: 13 inches.
Shipping Weight: 3,870 pounds with spade lugs, blocking, etc.
Color: Chassis and engine: Wallis gray; wheels: dark red.

Wallis Model OK

This tractor is essentially the same as the Model K, except a different style of water pump was put on the tractor to allow for a front crank for starting below the radiator.

Production Figures: 1922–1926: 2,444

Serial Numbers: 1922–1926: 23,200–40,000

Nebraska Tractor Test: Test No. 92 (April 1923)

Serial Number Tested: No. 23,273

Drawbar Horsepower: 16.28.

Drawbar Horsepower: Average 15; belt 27.

Drawbar Pull: 2 1/2 miles per hour, 2,600 pounds maximum; 2,000 pounds constant.

Type of Engine: Vertical four-cylinder, four-cycle, valve-in-head. Cast in block, with removable cylinder sleeves.

Bore and Stroke: 4 1/4x5 3/4 inches.

Normal rpm: 900 to 1000.

Piston Rings: Three 1/4-inch-wide rings on each piston.

Diameter of Piston Pin: 1 1/4 inch; two bearings in piston bosses. Diameter of inlet and exhaust valve-clear: 1 5/8 inches.

Crankshaft: Balanced chrome-vanadium steel, heat-treated; all bearings 2 1/4-inch diameter.

Belt Pulley: 18 1/2-inch diameter by 7-inch face, running 475 rpm. Located left-hand-side chassis, running forward.

Transmission: Wallis Special, enclosed; two speeds forward, one reverse.

Drive Wheels: 48-inch diameter by 12-inch face.

Three Removable Phosphor Bronze Back, Babbitt Lined Main Bearings. Front bearing 2 1/4-inch diameter by 2 3/4 inches long. Center bearings, 2 1/4-inch diameter by 3 1/4 inches long. Rear bearings, 2 1/4 inches diameter by 4 3/4 inches long.

Weight of Motor: 750 pounds.

Oiling System: Positive pump and splash.

Ignition: High tension magneto, with impulse starter. Bosch DU4.

Carburetor: Bennett 1 1/4-inch gasoline. Kerosene equipment, special. Model W5.

Governor: Hydraulic type, Wallis make.

Fuel Supply: To carburetor by gravity. Fuel tank: one for gasoline equipment. (Extra tank for kerosene.) Capacity: 20 gallons.

Cooling System: Enclosed, tubular type. Modine radiator. Water capacity: 5 1/4 gallons. Circulation: By centrifugal pump.

The Wallis Model OK.

Air Circulation: By belt-driven fan.

Clutch: Twin disc, three-plate type.

Two Front Wheels: 30-inch diameter by 8-inch face.

Frame: Wallis patented, boiler plate, "U" shape.

Wheelbase: 84 inches, tread 49 inches.

Total Width: 61 inches overall. Length: 132 inches overall. Turning radius; clear outside, 15 feet.

Height of Drawbar: 13 1/2 to 17 inches. Clearance at lowest point: 13 inches.

Shipping Weight: 3,880 pounds, including spade lugs, blocking, etc.

Retail Price: (1925) $1,390

Color: Wallis gray body and engine, with dark red wheels.

Wallis Certified Model 20-30

The Wallis 20-30 was also known as the "certified" tractor. The Wallis certification was a type of guarantee of the tractor's horsepower and workmanship.

Production Figures: 1926–1932: Unavailable
Serial Numbers: 1926–1932: 40,001–69,000
Nebraska Tractor Test: Test No. 134 (April 1927)
Serial Number Tested: No. 50470
Drawbar Horsepower: 19.8.
Belt Horsepower: 30.24.
Speeds: Low: 2 3/4 miles per hour. High: 3 1/3 miles per hour.
Type of Engine: Vertical four-cylinder, four-cycle, valve-in-head. Cast in block, with removable honed cylinder sleeves machined to an even wall thickness.
Bore and Stroke: 4 3/8x5 3/4 inches.
Motor Speed: Normal rpm 1,050.
Oiling System: Combination pressure metering and splash.
Ignition: High tension magneto, with impulse starter. Bosch ZR4.
Carburetor: Gasoline, kerosene, or distillate. Kingston Model L.
Vaporizer: Rodger's Fuel Saving.
Governor: Fly ball, variable speed.
Cooling System: Tubular-type radiator, enclosed. Water capacity: 6 3/4 gallons.
Circulation: By centrifugal pump.
Clutch: Three-plate type.
Belt Pulley: 19-inch diameter by 7-inch crown face, balanced, fiber faced, running 475 rpm. Located on left-hand side, running forward. Detachable.
Transmission: Wallis special, enclosed; two speeds forward, one reverse.
Drive Wheels: 48-inch diameter by 12-inch face.
Frame: Wallis patented, boiler plate, "U" shape.
Wheelbase: 84 inches, tread 49 inches.
Weight: 4,381 pounds.
Power: S.A.E. recommended rating, drawbar 20 horsepower, belt 30 horsepower.
Height Overall: 55 inches.
Length Overall: 131 1/2 inches.
Fuel Tank, Large: 20 gallons.
Auxiliary Gas Tank: 1 3/4 gallons.

The Wallis 20-30.

Vaporizer Water Tank: 1 3/4 gallons.

Traction Lugs: Special Wallis two-bolt 5-inch drop-forged steel spade lugs are standard; 6 inch also available at slight additional cost.

Turning Radius: 14 feet.

Retail Prices: (1927) $1,295; (1932) $1,125

Options (1932):

- Rice tractor with 12-inch extension rims and extension hubs, $1,200.00
- 6-inch extension rims, $28.00
- 12-inch extension rims, $100.00
- Power takeoff, $44.00
- Radiator V-shaped screen, $3.75
- Front wheel skid bands, $6.25
- Hand brake, $16.00
- Lighting equipment with generator, $60.00
- Wheel scrapers, $8.00
- Swinging drawbar, $5.00

Color: Wallis gray body and engine, with dark red wheels.

Wallis Certified Model 12-20

This tractor was called the Massey-Harris Model 12 from 1932–1935 and became the Pacemaker and Challenger (Row-Crop version) after the Massey-Harris takeover of Wallis. The Wallis "Certified" 12-20 Tractor is a little brother of the world-famous Wallis 20-30. It was built to meet the demand for a two-plow tractor.

Production Figures: 1929–1935: Unavailable

Serial Numbers: Standard 1929–1935: 100,000–107,000

      Orchard 1930: 200,000–200,402

      Industrial 1930: 250,001–250,026

Nebraska Tractor Test: Test No. 164 (June 1929)

Serial Number Tested: No. 100137

Drawbar Horsepower: 12.34.

Belt Horsepower: 20.32.

Engine: 3 7/8-inch bore, 5 1/4-inch stroke, 1,000 rpm. Vertical four-cylinder, four-cycle, valve-in-head. Cast in block with removable honed cylinder sleeves. Sleeves are machined on outside to maintain uniform thickness.

Crankshaft: Balanced, heat-treated. All bearings are 2 1/8-inch diameter. Connecting rod bearings 2 1/2 inches long. Main bearings have 9 1/2-inch total length.

Oiling System: Combination forced feed metering and splash system. Positive gear-type oil pump. Oil filtering device.

Ignition: High tension magneto with impulse starter. Bosch U4.

Carburetor: Gasoline, kerosene, or distillate. Kingston L3V.

Vaporizer: Rodgers.

Governor: Fly ball type. Kingston.

Cooling System: Tubular-type radiator. Centrifugal type water pump. 16-inch belt-driven, Timken mounted, fan. Capacity: 5 gallons of water.

Clutch: Twin disc, three-plate type.

Belt Pulley: 17-inch diameter x 6-inch crown face, balanced, 540 rpm, 2,400 feet per minute belt speed.

Transmission: Wallis special, enclosed. All gears running in bath of oil, three speeds forward, one speed reverse. Drop-forged gears, machine cut teeth, carburized and hardened.

Tractor Speeds: Low: 2 1/3 miles per hour. Intermediate: 3 1/3 miles per hour. High: 4 1/3 miles per hour. Reverse: 2 1/3 miles per hour.

Bearings: Anti-friction bearings used throughout. Ball and Timken tapered roller bearings.

The 12-20 Wallis Orchard Model.

Drive Wheels: 44-inch diameter by 10-inch face.
Front Wheels: 28-inch diameter by 5-inch face.
Frame: Wallis patented "U" shaped boiler plate frame.
Wheelbase: 78 inches. Tread 45 inches.
Shipping Weight: 3,431 pounds.
Power: 12 horsepower at drawbar, 20 horsepower on belt.
Height Overall: 51 inches.
Length Overall: 121 inches.
Fuel Tank, Large: 15 gallons.
Auxiliary Gas Tank: 1 3/4 gallons.
Vaporizer Water Tank: 1 3/4 gallons.
Turning Radius: 11 1/2 feet.
Retail Price: 1932 – $875.
1932 Options:
   • Orchard tractor, $905.00
   • 6-inch extension rims, $28.75
   • 10 inch extension rims, $65.75
   • Lighting equipment with generator, $60.00
   • Swinging drawbar, $4.50
   • 4-inch front wheel skid bands, $12.50
   Power takeoff (1 1/8 inch or 1 3/8 inch), $43.75
Color: Wallis gray body, with dark red wheels.

Massey-Harris General Purpose (GP) Four-Wheel Drive

In 1930, Massey-Harris introduced the first tractor developed by Massey-Harris engineers. It was the first major manufacturer to design and produce a four-wheel-drive tractor. Its design was advanced for its time, but its lack of power and Depression-era release time proved to be its downfall. The wheel tread was not adjustable on each tractor, so the tractors were offered from the factory with four wheel-width options—48 inch, 60 inch, 66 inch, and 76 inch. Massey also tried to promote the versatility of this tractor by offering orchard, railroad, golf course, and industrial models. This was the first Massey tractor available with optional electric starter or optional lights and generator. The 48-inch orchard model was the only four-wheel drive available with fenders.

Production Figures:1930–1936: Under 3,000

Serial Numbers:		
	1930:	300,001–300,428
	1931:	300,429–300,857
	1932:	300,858–301,287
	1933:	301,288–301,717
	1934:	301,718–302,146
	1935:	302,147–302,575
	1936:	302,576–302,999

Engine: 4-inch bore, 4 1/2 -inch stroke, 1,200 rpm. Vertical four-cylinder cast in block. L-head type. Hercules Model OOC.

Crankshaft: Double-balanced, heat-treated. Three bearings, total bearing length, 7 1/16 inches; 2-inch diameter.

Oil System: Dual system, force fed by gear pump and dip pan splash. Oil filtering device.

Ignition: High tension magneto with impulse starter. Bosch U4.

Fuel: Gasoline.

Air Cleaner: Massey-Harris, oil flushing.

Governor: Variable speed, fly ball type.

Carburetor: Zenith Model 94T0, 1 inch.

Cooling System: Tubular type radiator. Centrifugal-type water pump. 18-inch fan, mounted on Timken Bearings and driven by a V-belt.

Clutch: Twin disc, three-plate type.

Belt Pulley: 12-inch diameter, 6 1/2-inch crown face; balanced, removable, 800 rpm, 2,513 feet per minute belt speed.

Transmission: Massey-Harris special.

1930 Massey-Harris GP Four-Wheel-Drive Model.

Tractor Speeds: Low: 2.2 miles per hour; intermediate: 3.2 miles per hour; high: 4 miles per hour. Reverse: 2 1/2 miles per hour.

Brakes: Two, one for each front wheel, mounted on differential.

Drive Wheels: Four, 38-inch diameter, 8-inch face.

Wheelbase: 51 inches.

Tread: 60 inches, 66 inches, and 76 inches standard model. 48 inches orchard.

Clearance: 30 inches between axle and ground.

Turning Radius: Inside, without brakes 6 1/2 feet, with brakes 3 feet. Weight: 3,861 pounds.

Hitch: Swinging drawbar.

Rating: Belt 25 horsepower. Drawbar 16 horsepower.

Extra Equipment:

- Extension Controls to the seat of the drawn implement, giving full control of tractor.
- Lights, electric with generator and battery.
- Starter, electric with generator and battery.
- Power Takeoff, 545 rpm. Standard 1 3/8-inch spline connection, 1 1/8 inch furnished on special order.
- Open Wheels with wing lugs; also overtires and spade lugs.

Orchard Tractor Specifications

Turning Radius: 5 feet, with brakes.

Tread: 48 inches.

Weight: Approximately 3,750 pounds.

Fenders: Four steel fenders, with aprons, giving full protection.

Wheel Scrapers: Efficient, adjustable scrapers on all wheels.

Belt Pulley: Not furnished regularly on orchard model.

Extra Equipment:

- Extension Controls to the seat of the drawn implement, giving full control of tractor.
- Lights, electric with generator and battery.
- Starter, electric with generator and battery.
- Power Takeoff, 545 rpm. Standard 1 3/8 inch spline connection, 1 1/8 inch furnished on special order.

Retail Price: (1933) (All Tread Widths): $995.00

Options:

- 1933 Self-starter & lights, $81.25
- 1933 Power Takeoff, $21.90
- 1933 Belt pulley, $21.90
- 1933 Four extension rims, $43.75
- 1933 Power lift, $67.00

Nebraska Tractor Test: Test No. 177 (May 1930)

Serial Number Tested: No. 300089

Drawbar horsepower 15.64, belt horsepower 24.84. Retested Test No. 191 (May 1931)

Serial Number Tested: No. 302164

Drawbar horsepower 12.63, belt horsepower 20.11.

Color: Dark gray body with dark red wheels.

Massey-Harris Model 25 (Unstyled)

The Model 25 was an improved version of the 20-30 Wallis tractor. The Wallis name was dropped, but the Wallis U-frame design was retained. This was the first Massey tractor to move away from the Wallis gray color to a dark forest green color for the engine and chassis. Red wheels were retained.

Production Figures: 1932–1938: 14,112

Serial Numbers:

	1933:	69,001–69,699
	1934:	69,700–70,398
	1935:	70,399–71,097
	1936:	71,098–71,798
	1937:	71,799–72,804
	1938:	72,805–73,111

Rating: 26 drawbar horsepower, 41 belt horsepower.

Engine: Own, Model "25," 4 3/8-inch bore, 5 3/4-inch stroke, 1,200 rpm, four-cylinders, vertical, valve-in-head, removable, honed, alloy iron cylinder sleeves. (Probably cast by Continental.)

Cooling System: Tubular-type radiator, removable core, 18-inch-diameter fan, centrifugal water pump, capacity 6 U.S. or 5 Imperial gallons.

Fuel: Gasoline, kerosene, or distillate. Main tank capacity 24 U.S. or 20 Imperial gallons. Auxiliary tank capacity 1 3/4 U.S. or 1 1/2 Imperial gallons.

Lubrication: Engine: combination pressure-metering and splash system with in-line oil filter. Transmission: oil bath. Rear axle: oil bath. Chassis: high-pressure grease system.

Transmission: Selective sliding gear type. All gears are carburized and hardened. 1st reduction gears: spiral bevel; 2nd reduction gears: spur; final (3rd) reduction gears: spur.

Clutch: Single plate, twin disc, hand operated.

Belt Pulley: Fiber face type, 19-inch diameter x 7 1/8-inch crowned face, 525 rpm, 2,612 feet per minute belt speed. Spiral bevel gear drive. Wheels: Rear: 48-inch diameter x 12-inch face. Front: 30-inch diameter x 6-inch face.

Speeds: (Standard) Forward: 2 1/2, 3 1/4, 4 miles per hour. Reverse: 2 1/2 miles per hour. Overall Dimensions: Length, 135 inches; width, 65 1/2 inches; height over hood, 57 inches.

Wheelbase: 84 inches.

Tread: Rear, 53 1/2 , front, 50.

Outside Turning Radius: 13 feet.

Weights: Shipping: 4,919 pounds; field: 5,165 pounds.

Scrapers: Standard equipment for rear wheels.

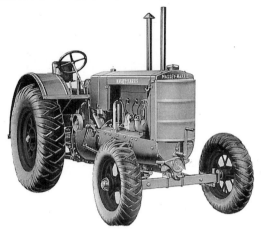

Massey-Harris Model 25.

Power Takeoff: (extra) 1 3/8 inch, 6B, S.A.E. spline, 545 rpm.
Ignition: Bosch U4 magneto.
Carburetor: Kingston Model L3L, 1 1/2 inch.
Governor: Kingston J8728.
Tires: Optional equipment: front 7.50x18 inches; rear 12.75x28 inches, 13.50x28 inches, 12.75x32 inches.
Nebraska Tractor Test: Test No. 219 (November 1933)
Serial Number Tested: No. 69,001
Drawbar horsepower: 24.92; belt horsepower: 44.24.
Color: Dark green engine and body, dark red wheels, yellow decals.
Retail Prices: (1937)
  • Model 25 on steel wheels: $1,275.00
  • Model 25 with rubber tires: $1,530.00
Standard equipment: fenders, radiator screen, rear wheel scrapers, belt pulley
Options:
  • Skid bands—front wheels, $8.75
  • Cowhide seat cover, $4.40
  • Cushion seat with back, $18.75
  • Power takeoff, $43.75
  • Swinging drawbar, $6.60
  • Belt guide, $7.50
  • 6-inch extension rim, $28.25

Massey-Harris Pacemaker Model PA (Unstyled)

The Massey-Harris Pacemaker was essentially the same tractor as the Model 12-20 Wallis. Again, as with the Model 25, the Massey-Harris name replaced the Wallis name and the color of the tractor was changed from a gray body to dark green with dark red wheels. The tractor was also offered in orchard and vineyard models.

Production Figures: 1936–1937: 2,837
Serial Numbers: 1936: 107,001–108,419
      1937: 108,420–109,837
      Orchard 1936 200,251–200,402
      Vineyard 1936: 200,001–200,250
Engine: Massey-Harris make. Four-cylinder; 3 7/8-inch bore, 5 1/4-inch stroke, 1,200 rpm. Vertical valve-in-head, removable honed alloy iron cylinder sleeves. Cast by Continental.
Power: Two- to three-plow capacity.
Crankshaft: Balanced, heat-treated. All bearings are 2 1/8-inch diameter. Connecting rod bearings 2 1/2 inches long.
Oiling System: Engine: combination pressure-metering and splash system with full flow in-line oil filter. Transmission: oil bath. Rear axle: oil bath. Chassis: high pressure grease system. Positive lubrication to timing gears, impulse starter, governor, valves, and rocker arms.
Ignition: High tension magneto with impulse starter. Bosch Model U4ED4.
Carburetor: Gasoline, kerosene, or distillate. New balance tube arrangement maintains proper fuel and air mixture. Idling and high speed adjustment. 1 1/4-inch Kingston.
Vaporizer: Fuel saving, Massey-Harris patent.
Air Cleaner: Massey-Harris automatic oil flush type.
Governor: Handy Model R02281-C. Variable speed, centrifugal type, enclosed and oiled by the pressure system.
Manifold: One-piece intake and exhaust.
Cooling System: Tubular radiator, removable core. 16-inch-diameter fan and centrifugal packless-type water pump driven by a "V" belt. 308-square-inch frontal radiator area.
Clutch: Single plate, twin disc, hand operated.
Belt Pulley: Fiber face type, 12-inch diameter x 6 1/4-inch crowned face, 831 rpm, 2610 feet per minute belt speed.
Steering Gear: High-grade, heavy-duty modern bus and truck-type. Irreversible.
Transmission: Selective sliding-gear type. All gears are carburized and

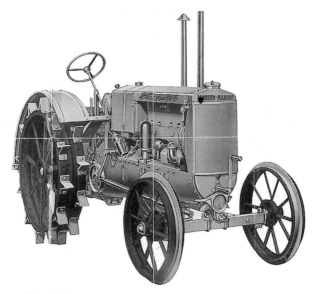

Massey-Harris Pacemaker.

hardened. First reduction gears: spur; second reduction gears: spiral bevel; final reduction gears: spur.

Tractor Speeds: 2.4, 3.3, 4.1, and 8.5 miles per hour. Reverse: 3.0.

Bearings: Anti-friction bearings used throughout. Ball and Timken-tapered roller bearings.

Drive Wheels: 44-inch diameter, 10-inch face.

Front Wheels: 28-inch diameter, 5-inch face.

Brakes: Hand operated, emergency or holding brake.

Rubber Tire Equipment: Front 6:00x16; rear 11:25x24. 12:75x24 available at extra cost.

Frame: Massey-Harris patented "U" shaped boiler plate frame.

Wheelbase: 78 inch. Tread 46 inch. Vineyard Model: 40-inch tread.

Length Overall: 122 inches. Width: 56 inches. Height over hood: 53 inches.

Fuel Tank, Large: 18 gallons.

Fuel Tank, Auxiliary: 1 5/8 gallons.

Vaporizer Water Tank: 1 5/8 gallons.

Turning Radius: 11 1/2 feet outside radius.

Weight: Shipping weight 3,695 pounds.

Fenders: Heavy construction, well braced. (Standard equipment)

Scrapers: Standard equipment for rear wheels.

Power Takeoff: (Extra Equipment) 1 3/8 inch, 530 rpm.

Hitch: Swinging drawbar, standard.

Nebraska Tractor Test: Test No. 266 (August 1936)

Serial Number Tested: No. 107484

Drawbar horsepower 16.21; belt horsepower 26.69.

Retail Prices: (1937)
- Model PA on steel wheels: $1,010.00
- Model PA on rubber tires: $1,200.00
- Model PA-Orchard on steel: $1,065.00
- Model PA-Orchard on rubber: $1,225.00

Standard equipment: fenders, belt pulley, brake, radiator screen, swinging drawbar

Options:
- Cowhide cover seat, $4.40
- Cushion seat with back, $18.75
- Power takeoff, $43.75
- 6-inch extension rims, $29.75
- Lights and generator, $60.00

Color: Dark green engine and body with dark red wheels, yellow decals.

Massey-Harris Challenger Model CH (Unstyled)

The Challenger was Massey's first row-crop tricycle tractor. It was based on the same engine and transmission as the Wallis 12-20 and Pacemaker tractors. An adjustable wide front end was offered as an option, but it is very rare to find one with that option today.

Production Figures: 1936–1937: 3,366

Serial Numbers: 1936–1937 130,001–133,366

A casting date is stamped on top of the transmission housing directly under the gas tank. This date will approximate the date of manufacture within a few weeks.

Rating: Full two to three plow. Two plows in any workable soil, three plows in all but hardest to work soil.

Engine: Own. 3 7/8-inch bore, 5 1/4-inch stroke, 1,200 rpm. Four-cylinder vertical, valve-in-head; removable honed alloy iron cylinder sleeves.

Cooling System: Tubular radiator. Capacity: 5 U.S. gallons. Removable core. 16-inch-diameter fan. Centrifugal, packingless water pump. Driven by "V" belt.

Fuel: Gasoline, kerosene, or distillate. Main tank capacity: 18 U.S. gallons. Auxiliary tank capacity: 1 5/8 U.S. gallons.

Lubrication: Engine-combination pressure-metering and splash system, with in-line oil filter; positive lubrication to timing gears, valve rocker arms, impulse starter, and governor.

Transmission: Oil bath.

Rear Axle: Oil bath.

Chassis: High pressure grease system.

Carburetor: 1 1/4 inch adjustable. Kingston.

Vaporizer: Massey-Harris. Patented. Fuel saving.

Air Cleaner: Massey-Harris, automatic oil flush type.

Governor: Variable speed. Centrifugal type. Enclosed and oiled by pressure system. Handy Model RD2231-C.

Ignition: High tension magneto with own impulse starter. Bosch Model U4-ED4.

Transmission: Selective sliding-gear type. All gears carburized and hardened. First reduction gears: spur; second reduction gears: spiral bevel; final (third) reduction gears: spur.

Clutch: Single plate, twin disc, hand operated.

Belt Pulley: Fiber faced, 12-inch diameter by 6 1/4-inch crowned face, 831 rpm. 2,610 feet per minute belt speed. Spiral bevel gear drive.

Steering Gear: High-grade, heavy-duty, modern truck and bus-type. Irreversible.

Massey-Harris Challenger.

Speeds: (Standard) Forward: 2.4, 3.3, 4.1, and 8.5 miles per hour. Reverse: 3 miles per hour.

Drive Wheels: Steel wheels, 52-inch diameter, open or closed type. Rubber tires (extra equipment) 9.00, 10.00, or 11.25x36 inches.

Front Wheels: Steel wheels, 24-inch diameter x 4 1/2-inch face. Rubber tires (extra equipment) 5.50x16.

Draw Bar: Swinging draw bar standard equipment. Fore and aft adjustment 7 1/2 inches. Swinging adjustment full swing or fixed in any position.

Wheelbase: 91 1/4 inches.

Tread: Adjustable 52 inches to 80 inches.

Weight: Shipping weight with open wheels less lugs, bolts, and skid bands: 3,520 pounds.

Turning Radius: Individual foot-operated brakes for each rear wheel pivot tractor on either wheel.

Overall Dimensions: Length: 129 1/4 inches; width: 78–88 inches; height over hood: 57 5/8 inches.

Special Equipment:

Power Takeoff: 1 3/8 inch; 6B; S.A.E. spline, 530 rpm.

Combined Power Lift and Power Takeoff, controlled by foot lever.

Retail Prices: (1937)
- Model CH on steel wheels: $1,025.00
- Model CH on rubber tires: $1,220.00
- Fenders, $20.00
- Power Lift, $45.00
- 150 lb. Rear Wheel Weight, $7.50
- 100 lb. Front Wheel Weights (2), $11.25

Nebraska Tractor Test: Test No. 265 (August 1936)

Serial Number Tested: No. 131,127

Drawbar horsepower: 16.29; belt horsepower: 26.21

Color: Dark (forest) green engine and chassis with dark red wheels, yellow decals.

Massey -Harris Twin Power Pacemaker (Styled)

The Twin Power Pacemaker was an improved styled version of the 1936 Pacemaker. Engine compression was increased. Twin Power was a new designation by Massey for increased belt horsepower. The tractor, when doing belt work, would have a twin power switch set, which would lock out the transmission and increase the governor-engine speed for more engine rpms and increased horsepower. The Nebraska Tractor Test on the belt increased 10 horsepower from its test of the unstyled Pacemaker to the styled Twin Power Pacemaker. The Twin-Power Challenger and Pacemaker were also the first Massey tractors in the traditional red bodies with straw-yellow wheels. This color combination would be used for the next 20 years.

A non-Twin Power version was available in a low-grade fuel model as the "Standard" Pacemaker.

Production Figures: 1937–1939: Unknown (probably fewer than 3,000)
Serial Numbers: Gas 1937–1939: 109,838–120,000
     Distillate 1937–1939: 120,001–130,000
     Orchard 1937–1939 200,403–201,000
     Vineyard 1937–1939 201,042–201,500
     Distillate Orchard 1937–1939 204,001–206,000
     Distillate Vineyard 1937–1939: 201,501–202,000
Rating: Three-plow power on drawbar, four-plow power on belt.
Engine: Own. 3 7/8-inch bore, 5 1/4-inch stroke. Four-cylinder vertical, valve-in-head; removable honed alloy iron cylinder sleeves.
Motor Speed: 1,200 rpm drawbar, 1,400 rpm belt.
Crankshaft: Balanced, heat-treated. All bearings are 2 1/8-inch diameter. Connecting rod bearings 2 1/2 inches long. Main bearings have 9 1/8-inch total length. Special formula steel.
Cooling System: Tubular radiator, capacity 4 1/6 Imperial Gallons. Removable core. 16-inch-diameter fan. Centrifugal, packingless water pump. Driven by "V" belt. 308 square inches frontal radiator area.
Fuel: 68–70 octane gasoline.
Main Tank Capacity: 15 Imperial Gallons.
Lubrication: Engine-combination pressure-metering and splash system, with in-line oil filter; positive lubrication to timing gears, valve rocker arms, and governor. Transmission: oil bath. Rear axle: oil bath. Chassis: high pressure grease system.
Carburetor: 1 1/4 inch adjustable. Zenith Model 62-AX9.

Massey-Harris Twin Power "Pacemaker" Orchard Model.

Air Cleaner: Oil flush type. Donaldson.

Governor: Variable speed. Centrifugal type. Enclosed and oiled by pressure system. Two-speed control. Kingston.

Ignition: High tension magneto with built-in impulse starter. Bosch Model MJB4A.

Transmission: Selective sliding-gear type. All gears carburized and hardened. First reduction gears: spur; second reduction gears: spiral bevel; final (third) reduction gears: spur.

Clutch: Single plate, twin disc, hand operated.

Belt Pulley: Fiber faced, 12-inch diameter by 6 1/4-inch crowned face. Spiral bevel gear drive.

Belt Speed: 831 rpm, 2,610 feet per minute belt speed. 969 rpm, 3,045 feet per minute.

Steering: Heavy-duty, irreversible.

Speeds: (Standard) Forward 2.4, 3.3, 4.1, and 8.5 miles per hour. Reverse 3 miles per hour.

Drive Wheels: Steel: 44-inch diameter, 10-inch face.

Rubber (Extra Equipment): 11.25x24; 12.75x24.

Front Wheels: Steel: 28-inch diameter x 5-inch face.

Rubber (Extra Equipment): 6.00x16.

Drawbar: Swinging drawbar standard equipment. Swinging adjustment full swing or fixed in any position.

Wheelbase: 78 inches. Orchard & Vineyard: 70 inches.

Tread: 46 inches. Vineyard: 40 inches.

Weight: Shipping weight with cast front and closed steel wheels and 5 inch 2 bolt steel spade lugs: 3,755 pounds.

Turning Radius: 11 1/2 feet outside radius.

Brakes: Hand-operated holding brake. Orchard & Vineyard: foot brakes.

Overall Dimensions: Length: 122 inches. Width: 56 inches (Vineyard 53 13/16 inches). Height over hood: 53 inches.

Fenders: Standard.

Scrapers: Standard.

Power Takeoff: 1 3/8 inches; 6B; S.A.E. spline, 530 rpm (extra equipment).

Combined Power Takeoff and Power Lift: None.

Nebraska Tractor Test: Test No. 294 (October 1937)

Serial Number Tested: No. 109,538

Drawbar horsepower: 20.30 belt horsepower: 36.78.

Retail Prices: (1938–1939)
- Model PA on steel: $975.00
- Model PA on rubber: $1,140.00
- Vineyard or Orchard PA on steel: $1,030.00
- Vineyard or Orchard PA on rubber: $1,235.00

Standard: Fenders, brakes, radiator screen, swinging drawbar, thermostat

Options:
- Cowhide covered seat, $4.40
- Cushion seat & back, $18.75
- Power takeoff, $43.75
- Muffler, $4.50
- Lights & generator, $60.00
- 75 lb. front wheel weights, $5.65
- 150 lb. rear wheel weights, $7.50
- 6-inch extension rims, $29.75

Color: Red engine and chassis with straw-yellow wheels, yellow decals.

Massey-Harris Twin Power Challenger (Styled)

The Twin Power Challenger was an improved styled version of the 1936 Challenger. Improvements included increased engine compression through domed pistons and the new twin-power feature discussed in the previous chapter.

The distillate version of the Challenger was designated the "standard" model.

Production Figures: 1937–1939: Unknown
Serial Numbers:
Gas 1937–1939: 133,367–140,000
Distillate 1937–1939: 140,001–144,000
Rating: Three-plow power on drawbar, four-plow power on belt.
Engine: Own. 3 7/8-inch bore, 5 1/4-inch stroke. Four-cylinder vertical, valve-in-head, removable honed alloy iron cylinder sleeves.
Motor Speed: 1,200 rpm drawbar, 1,400 rpm belt.
Crankshaft: Balanced, heat-treated. All bearings are 2 1/8 inch diameter. Connecting rod bearings 2 1/2 inches long. Main bearings are 9 1/8 inches long. Special formula steel.
Cooling System: Tubular radiator: capacity 5 U.S. Gallons. Removable core, 16-inch-diameter fan. Centrifugal, packingless water pump. Driven by "V" belt, 308 square inches frontal radiator area.
Fuel: 68–70 octane gasoline.
Main Tank Capacity: 18 U.S. gallons.
Auxiliary Tank: 1 5/8 U.S. gallons.
Lubrication: Engine-combination pressure-metering and splash system, with in-line oil filter; positive lubrication to timing gears, valve rocker arms, and governor. Transmission: oil bath. Rear axle: oil bath. Chassis: high pressure grease system.
Carburetor: 1 1/4-inch adjustable. Zenith Model 62-AX9.

Twin Power Challenger.

Air Cleaner: Oil flush type. Donaldson.

Governor: Variable speed. Centrifugal type. Enclosed and oiled by pressure system. Two-speed control. Kingston.

Ignition: High tension magneto with built-in impulse starter. Model Bosch MJB4A.

Transmission: Selective sliding-gear type. All gears carburized and hardened. First reduction gears: spur; second reduction gears: spiral bevel; final (third) reduction gears: spur.

Clutch: Single plate, twin disc, hand operated.

Belt Pulley: Fiber faced, 12-inch diameter by 6 1/4-inch crowned face. Spiral bevel gear drive.

Belt Speeds: 831 rpm, 2,610 feet per minute belt speed. 969 rpm, 3,045 feet per minute.

Speeds: (Standard) Forward: 2.4, 3.3, 4.1, and 8.5 miles per hour. Reverse: 3 miles per hour.

Drive Wheel: Steel: 52-inch diameter open or closed type.

Rubber (Extra Equipment): 9.00, 10.00, or 11.25x36 inches.

Front Wheels: Steel: 24-inch diameter x 4 1/2-inch face.

Rubber (Extra Equipment): 5.50x16 inches.

Drawbar: Swinging drawbar, standard equipment. Swinging adjustment full swing or fixed in any position.

Wheelbase: 91 1/4 inches.

Tread: Adjustable 52 to 80 inches (steel).

Weight: Shipping weight with cast front and closed steel wheels and 5 inch 2 bolt steel spade lugs: 3,860 pounds.

Turning Radius: Pivots on either wheel.

Brakes: One on each rear wheel.

Overall Dimensions: Length: 129 1/4 inches; width: 78–88 inches; height over hood: 57 5/8 inches.

Fenders: Extra equipment.

Power Takeoff: 1 3/8 inch; 6B; S.A.E. spline, 530 rpm (extra equipment).

Combined Power Takeoff and Power Lift: Foot operated (extra equipment).

Nebraska Tractor Test: Test No. 293 (October 1937)

Serial Number Tested: No. 132,578

Drawbar horsepower: 19.67, belt horsepower: 36.32

Retail Prices: (1938–1939)

- Model CH on Steel: $995.00
- Model CH on Rubber: $1,185.00

Standard: Brakes, swinging drawbar, thermostat, radiator screen, adjustable rear wheel tread.

Options:
- Fenders, $20.00
- Power Lift, $50.00
- Power Takeoff, $18.75
- 150 lb. Rear Wheel Weight, $7.50
- 100 lb. Front Wheel Weight (2), $11.25
- Muffler, $4.50
- Lights & Generator, $60.00

Color: Red engine and chassis with straw-yellow wheels.

General Purpose (GP) Four-Wheel Drive (Overhead Valve Model)

In an effort to improve the four-wheel-drive model, the company reintroduced it in 1936 with a different engine. The Hercules overhead valve model, however, produced little additional horsepower and the tractor was never very popular in an era when Row-Crop tractors were in demand. The hood was slanted slightly downward to the front on this model and the color was changed to a dark green body with red wheels.

Production Figures: 1936–1938: Unknown (probably around 1,000)

Serial Numbers: 1936–1938 303,001–355,000

Engine: 4-inch bore, 4 1/2 -inch stroke, 1200 rpm. Four-cylinder, vertical, valve-in-head removable cylinder sleeves. Hercules Model OHC.

Crankshaft: Double balanced, heat treated. Three bearings, total bearing length 7 1/16x2-inch diameter.

Oil System: Dual system, force fed by gear pump and dip pan splash. Latest type oil filter.

Ignition: High tension magneto with impulse starter.

Fuel: Gasoline, kerosene, distillate.

Vaporizer: Massey-Harris, patented, fuel saving.

Air Cleaner: Massey-Harris oil flushing.

Governor: Variable speed, centrifugal type.

Cooling System: Tubular-type radiator. Centrifugal-type water pump. 18-inch fan mounted on ball bearings and driven by a V-belt.

Clutch: Twin disc, single-plate type.

Belt Pulley: 12-inch diameter, 6 1/2-inch crown face, balanced, removable. 800 rpm, 2,513 per minute belt speed.

Transmission: Massey-Harris Special. Gears, drop-forged steel, machine cut teeth, carburized and hardened, enclosed in dust-proof case, running in oil.

Late General Purpose Four Wheel Drive.

Tractor Speeds: Low: 2.2 miles per hour; intermediate: 3.2 miles per hour; high: 4 miles per hour. Reverse 2 1/2 miles per hour.

Bearings: Ball and Timken throughout.

Brakes: Two, one for each front wheel mounted on differential.

Drive Wheels: Four, 38-inch diameter, 8-inch face.

Wheelbase: 52 1/2] inches.

Tread: 56, 60, 66, 76, and 48 inches for orchard work.

Clearance: 30 inches between axle and ground.

Turning Radius: Inside, without brakes 6 1/2 feet; with brakes 3 feet.

Hitch: Swinging drawbar.

Extra Equipment:
- Rubber Tires: 9.00x24 tires front and rear.
- Lights: Electric with generator and battery.
- Starter: Electric with generator and battery.
- Power Takeoff: 545 rpm. Standard 1 1/8-inch spline connection, 1 3/8-inch furnished on special order.
- Extension Controls to the seat of the drawn implement, giving full control of tractor.
- Power Lift Attachment

Nebraska Tractor Test: None.

Retail Prices: (1937)

- GP: All Treads on Steel: $1,245.00
- GP: All Treads on Rubber: $1,505.00

Options:
  - Power Takeoff, $6.50
  - Power Lift, $62.00
  - Extension Rims, $43.75

Color: Engine and chassis dark (forest) green with dark red wheels.

Massey-Harris Styled Model 25

The Model 25 was improved and styled in an effort to make the tractor similar in modern appearance to the Twin Power tractors. Not many Styled 25 tractors were made.

Production Figures: 1938–1940: Unknown (Probably fewer than 1,000)
Serial Numbers: A Gears 1938–1940: 73,112–85,000
    B Gears 1938–1940: 85,001–90,000
    Industrial 1938: 90,001-90,100
Horsepower: Rated drawbar: 26.44. Rated belt: 41.01. Maximum drawbar: 35.25. Maximum belt: 48.25.
Speeds: (Standard) 2 1/2, 3 1/4, 4 miles per hour. Reverse 2 1/2 miles per hour.
Overall Dimensions: Length: 135 inches. Width: 65 1/2 inches. Height over hood: 57 inches.
Shipping Weight: 4,919 pounds.
Outside Turning Radius: 13 feet.
Wheelbase: 84 inches. Rear tread, 53 1/2 inches; front tread, 50 inches.
Carburetor: 1 1/2-inch adjustable: gasoline, kerosene, or distillate.
Vaporizer: Massey-Harris, patented, fuel-saving.
Engine: Own. 4 3/8-inch bore, 5 3/4-inch stroke, 1,200 rpm. Four-cylinder, vertical, valve-in-head, removable honed cylinder sleeves.
Air Cleaner: Oil flush type.
Oiling System: Combination pressure-metering and splash system, with in-line oil filter.
Air Tires: Special order low pressure tires: front, 7.50x18; rear, 12.75x28.
Governor: Variable speed, centrifugal type.
Clutch: Single plate, twin disc, hand operated.
Transmission: Massey-Harris, enclosed, all gears carburized and hardened.
Wheels: Rear: 48-inch diameter by 12-inch face; front: 30-inch diameter by 6-inch face.

Massey-Harris Styled Model 25.

Belt Pulley: Fiber face type, 19-inch diameter by 7 1/8-inch crowned face, 525 rpm, 2,612 feet per minute belt speed, spiral bevel gear drive.

Cooling System: Tubular type, removable core, centrifugal water pump, capacity 5 Imperial Gallons.

Fuel Tanks: Main: 20 gallons; auxiliary: 1 1/2 gallons.

Brake: Hand-operated emergency or parking brake.

Scrapers: Standard equipment for rear wheels.

Power Takeoff (Extra Equipment): 1 3/8 inches; 6B; S.A.E. spline, 545 rpm.

Retail Prices:
- Model 25 on Steel: $1,275.00
- Model 25 on Rubber: $1,530.00

Standard: Fenders, belt pulley, swinging drawbar, brakes.

Options:
- Cushion seat and back, $18.75
- Power takeoff, $43.75
- Muffler, $4.50
- Lights and generator, $60.00

Massey-Harris Model 101 and 101 Super

In 1938, Massey-Harris introduced a newly designed tractor with a Chrysler industrial engine. The 1938 models are a "101" with no "Super" designation. The "Super" name was added in 1939, when the 101 Junior was introduced so the two 101 models would have their own clear model names. In 1940, the engine size was increased from 201 cubic inches to 217 cubic inches. The 101 was the first tractor built by a major tractor manufacturer that had electric starting as standard equipment. The standard tread models from Serial No. 358,245 to 358,918 had open (half-moon) side panels instead of the traditional louvered side panels used on earlier models.

Production Figures:

Years		Row-Crop	Standard
1938	(201 Engine)	1,084	602
1939	(201 Engine)	1,196	1,189
1940	(201 Engine)	1,004	2,267
1940	(217 Engine)	483	317
1941	(217 Engine)	993	681
1942	(217 Engine)	256	50

Serial Numbers:

Years		Row-Crop	Standard
1938	(201 Engine)	255,001–256,084	355,001–355,602
1939	(201 Engine)	256,085–257,280	355,603–356,791
1940	(201 Engine)	257,281–258,285	356,792–357,870
1940	(217 Engine)	258,286–258,768	357,871–358,187
1941	(217 Engine)	258,769–259,761	358,188–358,868
1942	(217 Engine)	259,762–260,017	358,869–358,918

1938 models can be distinguished from later models by their individual brake pedals on the left and right platforms, flattop fenders, a chrome hood badge, and cast rear wheels.

Rating: Full two- to three-plow drawbar power under normal plowing conditions, with three- to four-plow belt power by means of Twin Power control.

Engine: (1938–1940) Chrysler heavy-duty industrial. 3 1/8-inch bore; 4 3/8-inch stroke; six cylinders; L-head; 201.3-cubic-inch displacement. 6.7 to 1 compression ratio. (1940–1942) Chrysler heavy-duty industrial. 3 1/4-inch bore; 4 3/8-inch same stroke; six cylinders; L-head; 217.7-cubic-inch displacement. 6.5 to 1 compression ratio.

1938 Massey-Harris Model 101.

Engine Speeds: 1,500 rpm drawbar; 1,800 rpm high road speed and belt.

Weight: Row-Crop: 3,650 pounds. Standard: 3,435 pounds.

Cooling System: Tubular-type radiator equipped with bypass thermostat for quick warm-up and efficient operation in cold weather. Distributing tube directs coolest water directly to exhaust valve seats. 17-inch-diameter fan. Capacity 4 1/2 U.S. or 3 3/4 Imperial gallons.

Fuel: 68–70 octane gasoline.

Tank Capacity: Row-Crop: 18 gallons. Standard: 15 gallons.

Carburetor: Schebler 1 inch adjustable. Model TRX.

Lubrication: Full pressure lubrication provides circulation of oil to all vital parts; oil filter. Capacity 5 quarts. Positive lubrication to timing gears.

Governor: Handy-variable speed. Centrifugal type. Twin Power control.

Ignition: Battery-ignition system with automatic spark advance.

Transmission: Selective sliding-gear type. All gears are carburized and hardened. First reduction gears: spur; second reduction gears: spiral bevel; final (3rd) reduction gears: spur.

Speeds: 1,500 rpm: drawbar; 1st: 2.4; 2nd: 3.36; 3rd: 4.5 miles per hour. 1,800 rpm: drawbar; 4th: 17.35 miles per hour (rubber).

Clutch: Borg & Beck 11 inch, single plate, foot operated.

Belt Pulley: 13 1/2-inch diameter, 6 1/4-inch face, 1,500 rpm of motor 698 rpm 2,465 feet per minute. 1,800 rpm of motor 837 rpm 2,955 feet per minute.

Drive Wheel: Steel: Row-Crop: (closed) 50-inch diameter x 8-inch face, (open) 50-inch diameter x 1 15/16-inch face. Standard: 44-inch diameter x 10-inch face Front Wheel: Steel: Row-Crop: 22-inch diameter x 4 1/2-inch face. Standard: 28-inch diameter x 4 1/2-inch face.

Drive Wheel: Rubber: Row-Crop: 10:00x36, 11:25x36; Standard: 11:25x24, 12:75x24.

Front Wheel: Rubber: 5:50x16.

Wheelbase: Row-Crop: 89 1/2 inches. Standard: 78 inches.

Tread: Row-Crop: steel wheels: 52 inches, 80 inches; rubber wheels: 52 inches, 90 inches. Standard: steel wheels, 50 inches; rubber wheels, 52 inches.

Brakes: Individual rear wheel brakes permit pivoting on either rear wheel.

Fenders: Standard.

Power Takeoff: 1 3/8 inch; 6B; S.A.E. Spline. (Extra Equipment).

Combined Power Lift and Power Takeoff: Foot operated (extra equipment).

Nebraska Tractor Test: Row-Crop Test No. 306, Standard Test No. 307. (September 1938). Serial Numbers Tested: Row-Crop No. 255,257; Standard No. 355,064

Drawbar horsepower, 31.5; belt horsepower, 40.

Retested Test No. 377 (September 1941) with 217 engine Serial Number Tested: No. 258,390

Drawbar horsepower 34.6; belt horsepower 47.

Retail Prices: (1939)

Regular Equipment: Self-starter and battery, thermostat, fenders, platform, carburetor equipment for gasoline, full vision instrument panel with ammeter, oil gauge, and water temperature indicator, internal power takeoff shaft, 6x13 belt pulley, swinging drawbar, adjustable rear tread (Row-Crop only).
- 101 Row-Crop on rubber: $1,135.00
- 101 Standard on rubber: $1,125.00

Options:
- Power lift, $56.00
- Power takeoff extension, $15.00
- Lighting equipment, $16.00

Color: Tractor chassis: red. Wheels: straw yellow. Engine: black (replacement engine was aluminum color).

101 and 102 Junior Tractors

In April 1939, Massey-Harris introduced the 101 Junior tractor. It had a 124-cubic-inch Continental engine. Like the 101 model introduced in 1938, it departed from the older Wallis "U" frame design. Its price of $895 with starter and rubber tires was designed to compete with the lower-priced models of the other major manufacturers. In 1940, the 124-cubic-inch engine was replaced with a 140-cubic-inch Continental engine. The remainder of the basic tractor design remained unchanged until 1943, when the tractor was redesigned and fitted with a larger 162 Continental engine. 102 Junior models were originally designated as "102" for low-grade fuel (kerosene). As kerosene became less popular in the 1940s, the 102 merely designated an export version of the 101 Junior from the United States.

Production Figures and Serial Numbers by Year:

101 Junior Standard

Year	Serial Numbers	No. Built
1939	377,001–377,927	926
1940	377,928–379,549	1,621
1941	379,550–379,814	264
1942	379,815–379,854	39
1943	379,955–380,640	785
1944	380,641–382,568	1,927
1945	382,569–384,297	1,728
1946	384,298–385,640	1,342
	Total	8,632

101 Junior Row-Crop

Year	Serial Numbers	No. Built
1939	375,001–376,157	1,156
1940	376,158–376,999	841
1940	395,001–395,569	568
1941	395,570–397,636	2,066
1942	397,637–398,595	958
1943	398,596–399,682	1,086
1943	500,001–500,002	1
1944	500,003–502,433	2,430
1945	502,434–503,778	1,294
1946	503,779–505,512	1,733
	Total	12,133

Early 101 Junior.

102 Junior Standard (Kerosene)

Year	Serial Numbers	No. Built
1939	385,001–385,203	202
1940	385,204–385,449	245
1941	385,450–386,098	648
1942	386,099–386,661	562
1943	386,662–386,985	323
1943	390,001–390,007	6
1944	390,008–390,993	985
1945	390,994–391,912	918
1946	391,913–392,748	835
	Total	4,724

102 Junior Row-Crop (Kerosene)

Year	Serial Numbers	No. Built
1939	387,001–387,030	29
1940	387,031–387,126	95
1941	387,127–387,418	291
1942	387,419–387,600	181
1943	387,601–387,843	242
1944	387,844–388,239	395
1945	388,240–388,994	754
1946	388,995–389,171	176
	Total	2,163

By Engine Model

Model		Engine	Serial Numbers	No. Built
101 Jr.	RC	124 Continental	375,001–376,985	1,984
101 Jr.	Std.	124 Continental	377,001–378,713	1,712
101 Jr.	RC	140 Continental	376,986–376,999	13
101 Jr.	RC	140 Continental	395,001–399,682	4,681
101 Jr.	Std.	140 Continental	378,717–380,462	1,745
102 Jr.	RC	140 Continental (Kerosene)	387,001–387,844	843
102 Jr.	Std	140 Continental (Kerosene)	385,001–386,985	1,984
101 Jr.	RC	162 Continental	399,683–505,513	105,830
101 Jr.	Std.	162 Continental	380,463–385,641	5,178
102 Jr.	RC	162 Continental (Kerosene)	387,845–389,172	1,327
102 Jr.	Std.	162 Continental (Kerosene)	389,986–392,750	5,764

Note: The 124, 140, and 162 Continental engines are all the same size blocks so engines are interchangeable. Lots of the earlier models were upgraded through engine replacements by their owners.

Rating: Two-plow drawbar power under normal plowing conditions with added belt power by means of Twin Power control.

Early Engine: Continental heavy-duty industrial, 3-inch bore; 4 3/8-inch stroke; four-cylinder, L-head, 123.7-cubic-inch displacement; 6.75 to 1 compression ratio.

Mid Engine: Continental heavy-duty industrial, 3 3/16-inch bore, 4 3/8-inch stroke; four-cylinder, L-head, 140-cubic-inch displacement; 6.75 to 1 compression ratio.

Late Engine: Continental heavy-duty industrial, 3 7/16-inch bore, 4 3/8-inch stroke, four-cylinder, L-head, 162-cubic-inch displacement; 5 to 1 compression ratio.

Engine Speeds: 1,500 rpm drawbar. 1,800 rpm high road speed and belt.

Cooling System: Tubular-type radiator equipped with bypass thermostat for quick warm-up and efficient operation in cold weather. Cooling system employs a centrifugal, ball-bearing, packless sealed type water pump of large capacity. Cooling passages are so arranged in cylinder blocks as to ensure constant, positive cooling at all required points resulting in a uniform temperature throughout and freedom from hot spots. Capacity: 38 gallons per minute at 1,800 rpm. 16-inch-diameter fan. Capacity 11 quarts (U.S.)

Tank Capacity: 10 gallons.

Carburetor: Schebler 1 inch adjustable.

Governor: Pierce variable speed. Centrifugal-type Twin Power control.

Ignition: Battery-ignition system with automatic spark control.

Transmission: Selective sliding-gear type. All gears are carburized and hardened. First reduction gears: spur; second reduction gears: spiral bevel; final (3rd) reduction gears: spur.

Speeds: 1,500 rpm drawbar; 1st: 2.4; 2nd: 3.4; 3rd: 4.5 miles per hour, 1,800 rpm drawbar; 4th: 16.1 miles per hour (rubber)

Weight: Row-Crop: 3,250 pounds. Standard: 3,360 pounds.

Clutch: Borg & Beck 9 inch, single plate, foot operated.

Belt Pulley: 13 1/2-inch diameter, 6-inch face, 1,800 rpm of motor 837 rpm, 2,958 feet per minute.

Drawbar: Swinging or fixed position adjustable lateral and vertical.

Steering: Heavy-duty, irreversible.

Drive Wheel: Row-Crop: 8.36 rubber or 9.36. Standard: 10.28 or 11.28.

Front Wheel: Row-Crop: rubber 4.75x15. Standard: 5.00x15.

Wheelbase: Row-Crop: 83 1/2-inches. Standard: 78 inches.

Tread: Row Crop: rubber wheels 52 inches, 88 inches. Standard: rubber 52 inches.

Brakes: Individual rear wheel brakes permit pivoting on either rear wheel.

Fenders: Standard.

Power Takeoff: 1 3/8 inch; 6B; S.A.E. spline. (Extra Equipment).

Combined Power Lift and Power Takeoff: Foot operated (Extra Equipment).

Nebraska Tractor Test: Test No. 318 (124 engine) (May 1939)

Serial Number Tested: No. 375,186

Drawbar Horsepower 20.4; belt horsepower 26.2.

Retested October 1940, Test No. 359 (140 engine)

Drawbar Horsepower 24.6; belt horsepower 30.5.

Retail Prices: Standard Equipment: Self-starter and battery, thermostat, fenders, platform, full vision instrument panel with ammeter and oil gauge, internal PTO shaft, 6x13 1/2-inch belt pulley, carburetor equipment for gasoline, swinging drawbar, adjust rear wheel tread (Row-Crop only)

• 1939 (124 engine) on rubber, Row-Crop: $895.00
• 1941 (140 engine) on rubber, Row-Crop: $920.00
• 1941 (140 engine) Standard: $960.00

Options:
- Power lift, $56.00
- PTO extension, $15.00
- Lighting equipment, $11.00
- Muffler, $3.00
- Single front wheel, $80.00
- Wide front adjustable axle, $152.00

Color: Chassis: red; wheels: straw yellow; engine: black.

101 and 102 Senior Tractors

In 1942, the 101 Super was replaced by the 101 Senior tractor. The 101 Senior had a six-cylinder Continental engine instead of the Chrysler engine used in the 101 Super. The side panels were open and the air cleaner was moved from behind the grille to the side of the engine. The 102 tractors were essentially the same tractor, designed to burn low-grade (kerosene) fuel. The engine used in the low-grade fuel tractor was a 244-cubic-inch Continental, a little larger than the 226-cubic-inch Continental used in the gas versions. As kerosene became less popular, the later 102 models were merely an export model designation of the 101 Senior domestic models.

Production Figures and Serial Numbers by Year:

101 Senior Standard

Year	Serial Numbers	No. Built
1942	358,919–358,974	55
1943	358,975–359,456	481
1944	359,457–360,926	1,469
1945	360,927–362,519	1,592
1946	362,520–363,647	1,126
	Total	4,723

101 Senior Row-Crop

Year	Serial Numbers	No. Built
1942	260,018–260,429	411
1943	260,430–260,795	365
1944	260,796–263,019	2,223
1945	263,020–270,144	7,124
1946	270,145–272,506	2,360
	Total	12,483

101 Senior Row-Crop Tractor.

102 Senior Standard

Year	Serial Numbers	No. Built
1941	365,001–365,201	200
1942	365,202–366,061	859
1943	366,062–366,182	120
1944	366,183–367,352	1,169
1945	367,353–367,423	69
	Total	2,417

102 Senior Row-Crop

Year	Serial Numbers	No. Built
1942	265,001–265,043	42
1943	265,044–265,077	33
1944	265,078–265,286	208
	Total	283

Regular Equipment: Self starter and battery; thermostat; fenders; platform; carburetor equipment for gasoline; full vision instrument panel with ammeter, oil gauge and water temperature indicator; internal power takeoff shaft; 6x13-inch belt pulley; swinging drawbar; adjustable rear tread (Row-Crop only).

Rating: Three-plow drawbar power under normal plowing conditions with added belt power by means of Twin-Power control.

Engine: Heavy-Duty Industrial, 3 5/16-inch bore; 4 3/8-inch stroke; six cylinders; L-head; 226 cubic inch displacement. 6 to 1 compression ratio. Continental-built engine.

Engine Speeds: 1,500 rpm drawbar; 1,800 rpm high road speed and belt.

Cooling System: Tubular-type radiator equipped with bypass thermostat for quick warm-up and efficient operation in cold weather. Distributing tube directs coolest water directly to exhaust valve seats. 17-inch-diameter fan. Capacity 3 1/2 U.S. gallons.

Tank Capacity: 18 gallons, Row-Crop. 14 gallons, Standard.

Carburetor: Schebler 1 inch adjustable.

Governor: Novi, variable speed, centrifugal type, two-speed control on throttle quadrant.

Weight: Row-Crop: 3,760 pounds. Standard: 4,030 pounds.

Clutch: Borg & Beck 11 inch, single plate, foot operated.

Speeds: 1,500 rpm drawbar; (R.C.), 1st: 2.67; 2nd: 3.73; 3rd: 4.65 miles per hour. 1,800 rpm, drawbar; 4th: 12.25 miles per hour (rubber).

Belt Pulley: 13-inch diameter, 6-inch face. 1,500 rpm of motor 698 rpm, 2,465 feet per minute. 1,800 rpm of motor 837, rpm 2,960 feet per minute.

Drive Wheel: Steel: (closed) Row-Crop: 50-inch diameter x 8 inch. Standard: 44-inch diameter x 10-inch face.

Front Wheel: Steel: Row-Crop: 22-inch diameter x 4-inch face. Standard: 28-inch diameter x 4 1/2-inch face.

Drive Wheel: Rubber: Row-Crop: 11-38 or 12-38. Standard: 13-26.

Front Wheel: Rubber: Row-Crop: 5.50-16. Standard: 6.00-16.

Wheelbase: Row-Crop: 89 1/2 inches. Standard: 78 inches.

Tread: Steel Wheels: Row-Crop: 52 inches, 80 inches; Standard: 50 inches. Rubber Wheels: Row-Crop: 52 inches, 88 inches; Standard: 52 inches.

Fenders: Standard.

Power Takeoff: 1 3/8 inch; 6B; S.A.E. spline (Extra equipment).

Combined Power Lift and Power Takeoff: Foot operated. (Extra equipment) Distillate Model "102 Senior": Designed to burn distillate fuel with top efficiency. This model is fundamentally the same as the gasoline tractor except for the 244-cubic-inch engine; 3 7/16-inch bore, 4 3/8 inch stroke; compression ratio 4.85 to 1; engine speeds: drawbar, 1,600 rpm; belt, 1,900 rpm; "hot" manifolding.

Nebraska Tractor Test: Never tested.

Retail Prices: (January 1945)
• Row-Crop on rubber: $1,292.50
• Standard on rubber: $1,371.25

Options:
• Power lift, $70.40
• Power takeoff extension, $16.50
• Single front wheel, $117.00
• High arch adjustable front axle, $160.00
• 150 lb. rear wheel weights, $8.25
• Lighting equipment, $12.50

Color: Chassis: red; wheels: straw yellow; engine: black.

The General (Model GG)

In 1940, Massey-Harris did not have a low-cost, small tractor for small farmers and truck gardeners. As a result, it made a deal with the Cleveland Tractor Company of Cleveland, Ohio, to market in Canada the General tractor, which the Cleveland Tractor Company had introduced in 1939. The tractor was based on the HG Cletrac Crawler. The tractors sold by Massey-Harris dealers in Canada were identical to the General tractors sold in the United States by Cletrac dealers, except the Massey tractors had a serial number tag designating the tractor as built for the Massey-Harris Company. Massey sold the General tractor in 1940 and 1941, until introducing the 81 tractor, which replaced the General. The General was also sold in the United States by Montgomery Wards Stores as the Wards Twin Row. Eventually, Cletrac sold the tractor to the Avery Company and it became the Avery Model A.

Production Figures: Unknown.

Serial Numbers:	Years	First Serial No.
	1939	1FA001
	1940	5FA388
	1941	1FA0086–1FA0164
	1941	1FA1000
	1942	1FA6532

Engine: IXA and IXK Hercules Built.
Bore and Stroke: 3x4 inches.
Number of Cylinders: four.
rpm: 1,400.
Piston Displacement: 113.12 cubic inches.
Compression Ratio: 5.75 to 1.
Crankcase Oil Capacity: 5 quarts.
Cooling System Capacity (Thermo siphon type): 3 gallons.
Fan Diameter: 15 inches.
Fuel Tank Capacity: 12 gallons.
Ignition: high tension magneto.
Starting: manual.
Carburetor: Tillotsen YC2A or YC2B, 7/8 inch plain tube.
Drawbar horsepower, second gear: 12.5; belt horsepower: 18.
Clutch: Pedal-type, 9-inch single plate.
Transmission: Speeds: Low: 2.25 miles per hour, Second: 3.5 miles per hour, High: 6.0 miles per hour, Reverse: 2.5 miles per hour. Transmission case oil capacity: 10 quarts. Final drive oil capacity: 1 1/2 quarts.

The General Tractor.

Drawbar: Height: 13 inches, 15 1/2 inches, and 18 inches.

Wheels and Tires: Rear driving tires: 9x24 inches. Front (guide ring type) 5.50x16. Brakes: 5 1/2x2-inch face. Lever action, latch locking.

Dimensions: Length overall: 118 inches. Width overall (adjustable) 64–85 inches.

Height at top radiator: 55 inches. Gauge: Center to center of tires: 48–76 inches. Cultivating clearance: 23 inches. Wheelbase: 80 inches.

Shipping Weight: Approximate, equipped standard: 2,105 pounds.

Takeoff and Power Pulley: (special equipment) Diameter: 9 1/2 inches. Face: 5 1/2 inches. Speed: 1,055. Belt speed: 2,625 feet per minute. Takeoff: Size: 1 1/8 inches, 6 spline; Speed: 560 rpm. Oil capacity: 2 quarts.

Wheel Weights: (special equipment): 150 pounds each.

Nebraska Tractor Test: None.

Retail Price: (1940) $595.00

Color: Chassis, wheels, and engine: Cletrac yellow gold.

Massey-Harris Model 81 and 82

Massey-Harris introduced the Model 81 in 1941, in an effort to target small farms and small tractor needs with its own tractor, replacing the General tractor it had sold in Canada. The 81 used the same 124 Continental engine that Massey had previously used in its early 101 Junior tractors, but the 81 was built on a lighter frame than the 101 Junior's. 81 and 82 Standards were sold to the Royal Canadian Air Force and painted blue for use on Canadian air fields. The Model 82 was a low-grade fuel version of the Model 81 with a 140-cubic-inch engine.

Production Figures:
Model/Number Built

Year	81 RC	81 Std	82 RC	82 Std
1941	3,168	677	54	278
1942	186	79	219	173
1943	—	—	—	6
1944	10	23	—	—
1945	1,300	1,023	33	280
1946	1,937	771	118	421
Total	6,601	2,573	424	1,158

Serial Numbers:
Model 81

Year	Row-Crop	Standard
1941	400,001–403,167	425,001–425,677
1942	403,168–403,353	425,678–425,756
1943	—	—
1944	403,354–403,363	425,757–425,779
1945	403,364–404,663	425,780–426,802
1946	404,664–406,601	426,803–427,574

Model 82

Year	Row-Crop	Standard
1941	420,001–420,054	435,001–435,278
1942	420,055–420,273	435,279–435,451
1943	—	435,452–435,457
1944	—	—
1945	420,274–420,306	435,458–435,737
1946	420,307–420,425	435,738–436,159

Massey-Harris Model 81.

Regular Equipment: Rubber tires. Self-starter and battery. Full vision instrument panel with ammeter, oil gauge. Air cleaner, oil filter. Thermostat. Swinging drawbar. Adjustable rear tread 48 to 88 inches. Platform.

Rating: Two-plow drawbar power under normal plowing conditions; provision is made for increasing motor speed for belt work or top road speed.

Engine: Continental heavy-duty industrial, 3-inch bore, 4 3/8-inch stroke, four-cylinder, L-head, 124-cubic-inch displacement; 6.75 to 1 compression ratio.

Engine Speeds: 1,500 rpm drawbar; 1,800 rpm high road speed and belt.

Cooling System: Tubular radiator equipped with bypass thermostat for quick warm-up and efficient operation in cold weather. Cooling system employs a centrifugal, ball bearing, packless sealed-type water pump of large capacity. Cooling passages are so arranged in cylinder blocks as to ensure constant positive cooling at all required points, resulting in a uniform temperature throughout and freedom from hot spots. Capacity: 38 gallons per minute at 1,800 rpm. 16-inch-diameter fan. Capacity 100 quarts (U.S.).

Weight: Row-Crop: 2,535 pounds. Standard: 2,675 pounds.

Tank Capacity: 12 gallons.

Carburetor: Schebler 1 inch adjustable.

Governor: Pierce variable speed. Centrifugal type, two-speed control on throttle quadrant.

Speeds: At 1,500 rpm drawbar; (R.C.), 1st: 2.57 miles per hour; 2nd: 3.69 miles per hour; 3rd: 4.87 miles per hour. At 1,800 rpm 4th: 16.45 miles per hour.

Clutch: Borg & Beck 9 inch, single plate, foot operated.

Drive Wheels: Rubber only; 9-32 regular; 10-28 oversize.

Front Wheels: Rubber only; 4.00x15 (Std. Tread: 5.00x15).

Wheelbase: 82 1/2 inches.

Tread: 48 inches, 88 inches (Std. Tread: 48 inches).

Brakes: Individual rear wheel brakes permit pivoting on either rear wheel.

Extra Equipment: Fenders. Belt pulley attachment: Rockwood 9 1/2-inch diameter x 6-inch face at 1,800 rpm, speed belt pulley turns at 1,224 rpm, giving a belt speed of 3,044 feet per minute. Power takeoff attachment. Power lift.

Distillate Model "82": Designed to burn distillate with top efficiency. This tractor is fundamentally the same as the gasoline model except for larger 140 inch Continental engine with special "hot" manifolding. 3 3/16-inch bore x 4 3/8-inch stroke.

Nebraska Tractor Test: Test No. 376 (September 1941)

Serial Number Tested: No. 400,475

Drawbar horsepower 20.8; belt horsepower 27.

Retail Prices: (January 1945)
- Row-Crop on rubber: $803.00
- Standard on rubber: $833.00

Options:
- Power lift, $75.00
- Fenders, $16.00
- Belt pulley, $22.00
- Power takeoff, $17.00
- Lighting equipment, $13.00
- Muffler, $4.00
- Single front wheel, $99.00
- Adjustable high arch front axle, $168.00
- 1,501 lb. wheel weights, $8.00

Color: Chassis: red; wheels: straw yellow; engine: black.

Massey-Harris Model 201

In an effort to meet the demand for a high horsepower standard tread tractor, Massey-Harris introduced the Model 201 in 1940. It was equipped with a 242-cubic-inch Chrysler engine. Most of the 201 tractors were sold in western Canada and the wheat belt of the United States. Because of the wartime production curtailments, very few of the 200 series of tractors were made. Model 201 tractors had a heavy cast-iron grille.

Production Figures:

1940	340
1941	150
1942	13
Total	503

Serial Numbers:

1940	91,201–91,540
1941	91,541–91,690
1942	91,691–91,703

Note: Tractors with Chrysler engine No. T100-513 and Part No. 666010 cast on head are high-altitude models.

Rating: Full four-plow drawbar power under normal plowing conditions with added belt power by means of Twin Power control.

Engine: Chrysler heavy-duty industrial, 3 3/8-inch bore, 4 1/2-inch stroke, six cylinders; L-head; 241.5-cubic-inch displacement; 6.7 to 1 compression ratio.

Engine Speeds: 1,700 rpm drawbar; 2,000 rpm belt.

Massey-Harris Model 201.

Cooling System: Tubular-type radiator equipped with bypass thermostat for quick warm-up and efficient operation in cold weather.
Distributing tube directs coolest water directly to exhaust valve
seats. 18-inch-diameter fan. Capacity 3 3/4 Imperial Gallons.

Gas Tank Capacity: 21 Imperial Gallons.

Carburetor: Schebler 1 1/4 inch adjustable.

Lubrication: Full pressure lubrication provides circulation of oil to all
vital parts; oil filter. Capacity 4 1/4 Imperial quarts. Positive
lubrication to timing gears. Transmission: oil bath. Rear axle: oil
bath. Chassis: high pressure grease system.

Governor: Novi-Variable speed. Centrifugal type. Twin-Power control.

Speeds: Drawbar, rubber tires: 1st: 2.64 miles per hour; 2nd: 3.74
miles per hour; 3rd: 4.64 miles per hour. 4th: 12.33 miles per
hour. Reverse: 2.25 miles per hour. Steel Wheels: 1st: 2.45 miles
per hour, 2nd: 3.48 miles per hour; 3rd: 4.32 miles per hour; 4th:
11.47 miles per hour. Reverse: 2.09 miles per hour.

Clutch: Borg & Beck 11 inch, single plate, foot operated.

Belt Pulley: 13 1/2-inch diameter x 8 1/4-inch face, 1,700 rpm of
motor 713 rpm, 2,517 feet per minute. 2,000 rpm of motor 839
rpm, 2,962 feet per minute.

Drawbar: Swinging or fixed position, adjustable laterally 21 1/8 inch,
11 inches from ground on steel; 12 3/4 inch on rubber.

Weight: 6,435 pounds.

Drive Wheel: Steel: 48-inch diameter x 12-inch face.

Front Wheel: Steel: 30-inch diameter x 6-inch face.

Drive Wheel: Rubber: (special order) 13:50x28.

Front Wheel: Rubber: (special order) 7:50x18.

Wheelbase: 89 inches.

Tread: Steel wheels: 53 1/2 inches. Rubber wheels: 55 inches.

Brakes: Individual rear wheel brakes or locked together for master
brake control.

Fenders: Standard.

Power Takeoff: 1 3/8 inches; 6B; S.A.E. spline (Extra Equipment). 20
5/8 inches above drawbar.

Nebraska Tractor Test: None.

Retail Prices:

Regular Equipment: Self-starter, battery ignition, full vision instrument panel with ammeter, muffler, thermostat, oil gauge, water
temperature indicator, fenders, platform, swinging drawbar hitch,
8 1/4x13 1/2 belt pulley, internal power takeoff shaft, carburetor
equipment for gasoline

- June 1941, with rubber tires: $1,740.00

Options:

- Power takeoff, $40.00
- Lighting equipment, $11.00
- 150 lb. wheel weights, $8.00
- Distillate option, $100.00

Color: Chassis: red; wheels: straw yellow; engine: black.

Massey-Harris Model 202

At the same time the 201 was introduced, a Model 202 was introduced with a larger, 290-cubic-inch Continental engine. The chassis of the 201s, 202s, and 203s were basically the same. Only 223 of the 202 tractors were produced.

Production Figures:

1940	1
1941	180
1942	42
Total	223

Serial Numbers:

1940	95,001
1941	95,002–95,181
1942	95,182–95,223

Regular Equipment: Self-starter; battery ignition; muffler; thermostat; oil gauge; instrument panel with ammeter and temperature indicator; fenders; platform; drawbar hitch; belt pulley; carburetor equipped for gasoline.

Rating: Full four–five-plow drawbar power under all normal conditions. Added belt power by means of Twin-Power control.

Engine: Continental six-cylinder L-head type. 3 3/4 inch bore; 4 3/8 inch stroke; 290 cubic inch displacement. 5.7 to 1 compression ratio.

Engine Speeds: 1,700 rpm drawbar; 2,000 rpm belt.

Cooling System: Tubular-type radiator with bypass thermostat for quick warm-up and efficient cold weather operation. Capacity: 18 quarts. Water Jackets: Full length. Fuel Tank Capacity: 25 gallons.

Carburetor: Schebler 1 1/4 inch adjustable.

Air Cleaner: Oil flush type. United.

Lubrication: Full pressure lubrication provides circulation of oil to all vital parts; removable cartridge oil filter. Capacity 1 3/4 gallons. Positive lubrication to timing gears. Transmission: oil bath. Rear axle: oil bath. Chassis: high pressure grease system.

Governor: Pierce centrifugal type. Twin-Power control.

Ignition: Battery-ignition system with automatic spark advance.

Speeds: Low gear: 2.46 miles per hour; 2nd: 3.51 miles per hour; 3rd: 4.32 miles per hour; 4th: 12.7 miles per hour. Reverse: 2.1 miles per hour.

Clutch: Borg & Beck 11-inch single dry disc-type.

Belt Pulley: 13 1/2-inch diameter x 8-inch face. 809 rpm at 2,000 engine rpm. Fiber face type.

Massey-Harris Model 202.

Drive Wheels: Rubber, 14x30. Front Wheels: Rubber, 7.50x18.
General Dimensions: Wheelbase: 89 inches. Tread: front, 50 inches; rear, 55 inches. Width: 69 inches. Length: 139 1/2 inches. Height: 59 1/4 inches.
Weight: 6,500 pounds.
Brakes: Individual rear wheel brakes, may be locked together.
Power Takeoff: 1 3/8 inch; 6B; S.A.E. spline (Extra Equipment) 20 5/8 inches above drawbar.
Nebraska Tractor Test: None.
Retail Price: June 1941 with rubber tires: $1,795.00
Options:
  • Power takeoff, $40.00
  • Lighting equipment, $11.00
  • 50 lb. wheel weights, $8.00
Color: Chassis: red; wheels: straw yellow; engine: black.

Massey-Harris Model 203

The Model 203 was introduced in 1940 as a distillate model of the 201 and 202, with a larger 330 Continental six-cylinder engine. In 1944, a gasoline version was offered and was the primary model made instead of distillate. The early 203 tractors have a heavy cast-iron grille. Later models had the lighter, stamped steel (tin) grilles.

Production Figures:

Year	Figure
1940	27
1941	336
1942	310
1943	133
1944	954
1945	—
1946	474
1947	723
Total	2,957

Serial Numbers:

Years	Model 203	Model 203G
1940	98,001–98,027	—
1941	98,028–98,363	—
1942	98,364–98,673	—
1943	98,674–98,806	—
1944	98,807–99,688	95,224–95,294
1945	—	—
1946	99,68–100,119	95,295–95,337
1947	100,120–100,131	95,338–96,065

Regular Equipment: Self-starter; battery ignition; muffler; thermostat; oil gauge; instrument panel with ammeter and temperature indicator; fenders; platform; drawbar hitch; belt pulley; carburetor equipped for gasoline.

Rating: Full four–five-plow drawbar power under all normal conditions. Added belt power by means of Twin-Power control.

Engine: Continental six-cylinder L-head type. 4-inch bore; 4 3/8-inch stroke; 330-cubic-inch displacement. 5.86 to 1 compression ratio.

Engine Speed: 1,700 rpm drawbar. 2,000 rpm belt.

Cooling System: Tubular-type radiator with bypass thermostat for quick warm-up and efficient cold weather operation. Capacity: 22 quarts. Water jackets: full length.

Gasoline Tank Capacity: 24 gallons.

Massey-Harris Model 203.

Carburetor: Schebler 1 1/4 inch adjustable.

Air Cleaner: Oil flush type. United.

Lubrication: Full pressure lubrication provides circulation of oil to all vital parts; removable cartridge oil filter. Capacity 1 3/4 gallons. Positive lubrication to timing gears. Transmission: oil bath. Rear axle: oil bath. Chassis: high pressure grease system.

Governor: Pierce Centrifugal type, variable speed, two-speed control on throttle quadrant.

Ignition: Battery ignition system with automatic spark advance.

Speeds: Low gear: 2.48 miles per hour; 2nd: 3.53 miles per hour; 3rd: 4.35 miles per hour; 4th: 12.78 miles per hour. Reverse: 2.12 miles per hour.

Clutch: Borg & Beck 11 inch single dry disc-type.

Belt Pulley: 13 1/2-inch diameter x 8 1/4-inch face. 810 rpm at 2,000 engine rpm. Fiber face type.

Drive Wheels: Rubber: 14x30 or 15x30. Front Wheels: Rubber: 7.50x18.

General Dimensions: Wheelbase: 89 inches. Tread front: 50 inches; rear: 55 inches. Width: 69 inches. Length: 139 1/2 inches. Height: 59 1/4 inches.

Weight: 6,605 pounds.

Power Takeoff: 1 3/8 inches; 6B; S.A.E. spline. (Extra Equipment).

Distillate Model: "203-D"; Designed to burn distillate fuel with top efficiency, the distillate tractor is fundamentally the same as the gasoline model except for compression ratio 4.85 to 1; special "hot" manifolding.

Nebraska Tractor Test: None.

Retail Price: January 1945 (on rubber): $1,895.00

Options:
- Power takeoff, $18.00
- Lighting equipment, $13.00
- 150 lb. wheel weights, $8.00

Color: Chassis: red; wheels: straw yellow; engine: black.

Massey-Harris Model 20

In connection with the company's 100th anniversary in 1947, Massey-Harris engineers designed an entirely new line of tractors. The Model 20 was part of this new lineup even though its design was the same as the Model 81 that preceded it. The 20 was offered for only two years and was replaced in 1948 by the Model 22 when hydraulics were introduced.

Production Figures:

1946–1947	4,367
1948	3,564
Total	7,931

By Model:

20 Std Gas	1,660
20 RC Gas	4,198
20 K Std	1,430
20 K RC	643
Total	7,931

Serial Numbers:

Model 20 RC

1946	1,001–1,579
1947	1,580–3,583
1948	3,584–5,195

Model 20 Std

1946	1,001
1947	1,002–2,229
1948	2,230–2,661

Model 20 K Std

1947	1,001–1,818
1948	1,819–2,431

Model 20 K RC

1947	1,001–1,353
1948	1,354–1,644

Engine: (Continental Built) Cylinders: four; Bore: gasoline 3 inches, low-grade fuel 3 3/16 inches; Stroke: 4 3/8 inches; Speed rpm Drawbar, 1,500; Speed rpm Belt, 1800; Displacement: gasoline 124: low-grade fuel 140 cubic inch; ignition: battery; spark plug gap (Autolite B7 18 MM) -.025 inch; valve clearance int. and ex., .014 inch.

Massey-Harris Model 20.

Belt Pulley: Diameter: 9 1/2 inches; Face: 6 1/4 inches; rpm: 1,020 at 1,500 engine speed, 1,224 at 1,800 engine speed; belt speed (feet/minute): 3,040 at 1,800 rpm, 2,540 at 1,500 rpm.

Power Takeoff: Spline size 1 3/8 inches; Speed 1,500 engine rpm, 551 rpm; Speed 1,800 engine rpm, 661 rpm; Height from ground: 25 1/2 inches.

Foot Brakes: Disc-type foot operated.

Transmission: (four speed) 10x28 tire. 1st: 2.45 miles per hour; 2nd: 3.51 miles per hour; 3rd: 4.62 miles per hour; 4th (1,800 rpm): 13.02 miles per hour. Reverse: 3.0 miles per hour.

Wheels and Tread: Front Wheels: Tire Size: 4.00x15 (RC) 5.00x15 (Std); Rear Wheels: Tire Size: 8-32, 9-32 (RC) 8-32 10-28 (Std); Tread rear: 48-88 (RC) 48 (Std); Tread front: 45 3/4 inches.

General Dimensions: Over Tire   End of Drawbar
Length (Overall)
  Std   113 3/8 inches + 5 1/8 inches
  RC   113 3/8 inches + 5 1/8 inches
Width (Overall)
  Std   56 1/4 inches
  RC   81 1/2 inches over end of axles

Height (Overall)
  Std   67 3/8 inches over steering wheel
  RC   66 1/8 inches
Drawbar (Adjustable)
Vertical   7 5/8 inches   9 3/16 inches to each side of
                                          center
Ground Clearance
  RC & Std   11 1/2 inches to drawbar pin
Turning Radius
  Std   10 feet
  RC with brakes   86 1/2 inches at 48-inch tread
Capacities: Main fuel tank: 12 gallons; Auxiliary fuel tank (low grade
    fuel models): 1 gallon.
Water Cooling System: 2-3 U.S. gallons (2 1/3 Imperial gallons).
Engine Oil Pan: 4 U.S. quarts (.84 Imperial gallons); Belt pulley hous-
    ing: 3 quarts. Transmission case: 2 gallons. Differential case: 4
    gallons. Steering gear housing: 1 quart.
Weight: Row-Crop: 2,535 pounds. Standard: 2,675 pounds.
Nebraska Tractor Test: None
Retail Price: (1947) $1,296.00
Options:
      • Adjustable high arch wide front, $150.00
      • Single front wheel, $60.00
      • Velvet ride seat, $28.00
      • Belt pulley, $33.00
      • Power lift, $112.00
      • Lights, $19.00
Color: Chassis: red; wheels: straw yellow; engine: black.

Massey-Harris Model 22

The 22 replaced the 20 in the tractor lineup in 1948. The 22's improvements over the 20 included a larger, 140-cubic-inch engine and hydraulics as standard equipment. The 22 was also the first Massey-Harris tractor to offer an optional three-point hitch.

Production Figures: (All Models)

1948	886
1949	5,387
1950	3,917
1951	4,797
1952	2,194
1953	14
Total	17,195

Serial Numbers: (Located on plate mounted at rear of left frame member. Also stamped on top center of transmission housing.)

Model 22 RC

1948	1,001–2,095
1949	2,096–4,579
1950	4,580–7,623
1951	7,624–10,136
1952	10,137–10,783
1952	20,001–20,584
1953	20,585–20,623

Model 22 Std

1948	1,001–1,541
1949	1,542–3,207
1950	3,208–4,532
1951	4,533–5,716
1952	5,717–6,253
1952	20,001–20,584
1953	20,585—20,623

Model 22 K RC

1948	1,001–1,153
1949	1,154–1,335
1950	1,336–1,557
1951	1,558–1,775
1952	1,776–1,827
1952	20,001–20,584
1953	20,585–20,623

Massey-Harris Model 22.

Model 22 K Std

1948	1,001–1,316
1949	1,317–1,487
1950	1,488–1,569
1951	1,570–1,747
1952	1,748–1,823
1952	20,001–20,584
1953	20,585–20,623

Engine: (Continental Built) Cylinders: four; Bore: gasoline 3 3/16 inches, low-grade fuel 3 3/16 inches; Stroke: 4 3/8 inches; Speed rpm Drawbar, 1,500; Speed rpm Belt, 1,800; Displacement: gasoline 140, low-grade fuel 140 cubic inches; Pounds compression, cranking speed: gasoline: 110 minimum to 120 maximum, low-grade models, 80 minimum to 90 maximum; Ignition: Exide battery; spark plug gap (Autolite B7 18 MM): .025 inch; Valve clearance int. and ex.: .014 inch; carburetor: Marvel Schebler T5X34; Autolite positive ground 6-volt electrical system.

Belt Pulley: Diameter: 9 1/2 inches; Face: 6 1/4 inches; rpm: 1,020 at 1,500 engine speed, 1,224 at 1,800 engine speed; belt speed (feet/minute): 3,040 at 1,800 rpm, 2,540 at 1,500 rpm.

Power Takeoff: Spline size 1 3/8 inches; Speed 1,500 engine rpm, 551 rpm; Speed 1,800 engine rpm, 661 rpm; Height from ground: 25 1/2 inches; Left of center: 3 1/4 inches; Ahead of drawbar pin: 14 inches.

Weight: 2,840 pounds (without fluids and driver).

Transmission: (four speed) Row-Crop 9x32 and 10x28 tires, Standard 10x28 tire.

	9x32 tire	10x28 tire
1st	2.57 miles per hour	2.45 miles per hour
2nd	3.69 miles per hour	3.51 miles per hour
3rd	4.85 miles per hour	4.62 miles per hour
4th	13.68 miles per hour	13.02 miles per hour
Reverse	2.57 miles per hour	2.45 miles per hour

Wheels (Front):

RC	4.00x15
Std	5.00x15

Tread front: 45 3/4 inches

Tire size:	9-32	10-28	10-28
Tread rear:	48	8848	

General Dimensions: Over Tire   End of Drawbar

Length (Overall)

Std	113 3/8 inches + 5 1/8 inches
RC	113 3/8 inches + 5 1/8 inches

Width (Overall)

Std	56 1/4 inches
RC	81 1/2 inches over end of axles

Height (Overall)

Std	67 3/8 inches over steering wheel
RC	66 1/8 inches

Ground Clearance

RC and Std	11 1/2 inches to drawbar pin

Turning Radius

Std	10 feet
RC with brakes	86 1/2 inches at 48-inch tread

Capacities: Main fuel tank: 13 gallons; Auxiliary fuel tank (low-grade fuel models): 1 gallon.

Water Cooling System: 2 3/4 U.S. Gallons (2 1/3 Imperial Gallons).

Engine Oil Pan: 5 quarts (including filter); Belt pulley housing: 1 gallon; Transmission case/differential case: 5 1/4 gallons; Steering gear housing: 1 pound.

Standard Equipment: Self-starter, fenders, muffler, velvet ride seat, swinging drawbar.

Nebraska Tractor Test: Test No. 403 (October 1948)

Serial Number Tested: # 22GR1019

Drawbar horsepower 22.87; belt horsepower 31.05.

Retail Prices: (March 1951)

    22 Standard: $1,461.00

    22 Row-Crop: $1,434.00

Options:

- Hydraulic lift, $154.00
- 3-point hitch, $66.00
- Long rear axles for 112-inch tread, $52.00
- Hour meter, $27.00
- Belt pulley, $39.00
- Power takeoff, $26.00
- Lights, $22.00
- Single front wheel, $152.00
- High arch adjustable front axle, $222.00
- 150 lb. rear wheel weight, $17.00
- Pair 90 lb. front front frame weights, $29.00
- 80 lb. front wheel weight, $12.00

Color: Frame and engine: red, wheels: straw yellow.

Massey-Harris Model 30 Standard.

Massey-Harris Model 30

The Model 30 replaced the 101 Junior in 1947 as part of the new lineup of tractors introduced for the 100th anniversary of Massey-Harris. It retained the Continental 162-cubic-inch engine that the 101 Junior used in its last few years of production. The Model 30 proved to be a very popular tractor in the early 1950s and was outsold by only the Model 44 in the United States and Canada.

Production Figures:

1946	2
1947	3,888
1948	5,868
1949	6,114
1950	7,072
1951	6,376
1952	3,094
1953	4
Total	32,418

Serial Numbers: (Located on plate mounted at rear of left frame member. Also stamped on top center of transmission housing.)

Model 30 Std

1946	1,001
1947	1,002–2,119
1948	2,120–3,193
1949	3,194–5,566
1950	5,567–7,490
1951	7,491–8,695
1952	8,696–9,337
1952	30,001–30,595
1953	30,596–30,600

Model 30 RC

1946	1,001
1947	1,002–3,385
1948	3,386–6,824
1949	6,825–9,344
1950	9,345–13,815
1951	13,816–17,933
1952	17,934–19,382
1952	30,001–30,595
1953	30,596–30,600

Massey-Harris Model 30.

Model 30 K Std	
1947	1,001–1,893
1948	1,894–3,250
1949	3,251–3,530
1950	3,531–3,860
1951	3,861–4,170
1952	30,001–30,595
1953	30,596–30,600
Model 30 K RC	
1947	1,001–1,224
1948	1,225–2,009
1949	2,010–2,392
1950	2,393–2,718
1951	2,719–3,179
1952	30,001–30,595
1953	30,596–30,600

Engine: (Continental Built) Cylinders: four; Bore: 3 7/16 inches; Stroke: 4 3/8 inches; Speed: Belt pulley range (twin power) Engine, no load: 1,947 to 1,955 rpm; Engine, full load: 1,800 rpm; rpm Regular (Drawbar) Engine, no load: 1,720 to 1,728 rpm; Engine, full load: 1,500 rpm. Displacement: 162 cubic inches; Ignition: battery; spark plug gap (30) Autolite B7: .025 inches;

spark plug gap (30K) Champion 8 Commercial or Autolite B7 18 MM: .025 inch; Compression ratio: 6.23; Pounds compression cranking speed: Gasoline: 115 minimum, 120 maximum, Low grade: 85 minimum, 90 maximum; Valve clearance, intake and exhaust (hot setting): .014; Carburetor: Marvel Schebler, TSX 308; Electrical system: 6-volt positive ground, Autolite.

Belt Pulley: Diameter: 13 1/2 inches; Face: 6 1/4 inches; Speed: Belt pulley rpm (twin power), No load: 905 to 910 rpm; Full load: 838 rpm; Belt pulley regular (drawbar), No load: 800 to 805 rpm; Full load: 698 rpm. Belt speed (regular) 2,465 feet per minute; Belt speed (Twin power) 2,960 feet per minute.

Power Takeoff: Spline size: 1 3/8 inches; Speed, no load: 632 to 634 at 1,720 to 1,728 engine rpm; Speed, full load: 551 at 1,500 engine rpm; Height from ground (Std model): 32 1/2 inches; Height from ground (RC model): 36 5/16 inches; Left of center: 3/8 inches; Ahead of drawbar pin: 13 7/8 inches.

Transmission: (Row-Crop)

Rubber tires	10x38	11x38
1st	2.58 miles per hour	2.67 miles per hour
2nd	3.61 miles per hour	3.73 miles per hour
3rd	4.51 miles per hour	4.66 miles per hour
4th	6.31 miles per hour	6.52 miles per hour
5th	12.63 miles per hour	13.06 miles per hour
Reverse	2.93 miles per hour	3.02 miles per hour

Transmission: (Standard)

Rubber tires	11x28
1st	2.19 miles per hour
2nd	3.06 miles per hour
3rd	3.82 miles per hour
4th	5.35 miles per hour
5th	10.71 miles per hour
Reverse	2.48 miles per hour

Front wheels, tire size (rubber tires):

Std	5.00x15
RC	5.00x15

Rear wheels, tire size (rubber tires):

Std	11x28
RC	10x38

Tread, rear (rubber tires):

Std	52 inches
RC	52, 88 inches

Length (overall):

Std	125 inches
RC	127 inches

Width (overall):

Std	64 1/16 inches
RC	69 inches

Height (over steering wheel):

Std	73 inches
RC	79 inches

Weight (with gas, oil, and water):

Std	3,584 pounds
RC	3,468 pounds

Capacities: Main fuel tank: 19 gallons; Auxiliary fuel tank: 1 1/2 gallons; Water cooling systems: 3 gallons; Engine oil pan: 4 quarts; Transmission case: 13 gallons; Steering gear housing: 1 quart; Filter: 4/5 quart.

Nebraska Tractor Test: Test No. 409 (May 1949)

Serial Number Tested: # 30GR5172

Drawbar horsepower 26.24; belt horsepower 34.18.

Retail Prices: (February 1951)

Standard Equipment: Self-starter, velvet ride seat, fenders, muffler, belt pulley.

- Standard Tread: $1,832.00
- Row-Crop: $1,754.00

Options:

- Hydraulic lift, $168.00
- Power takeoff, $26.00
- Lights, $24.00
- Single front wheel, $199.00
- High arch adjustable wide front, $246.00
- Long rear axles for 112 inch tread, $70.00
- Hour meter, $27.00
- 150 lb. rear wheel weight, $17.00
- 80 lb. front wheel weight, $12.00

Color: Chassis and frame: red; engine (1947): black; engine (1948–1953): red; wheels: straw yellow.

Massey-Harris Model 44
(Gas, Kerosene, LP, and Diesel)
(Also known as Model 44-4)

The Model 44 was the most popular Massey-Harris tractor. More 44s were built in the United States than any other Massey-Harris tractor. The 44 and 55 were the first Massey-Harris tractors offered in LP and diesel versions. The LP, diesel, gas, and kerosene all used the same basic 260-cubic-inch Continental-built engine block with modifications for the various fuel types. The 44 was also the first Massey tractor to have an optional live PTO hand clutch. The 260-cubic-inch overhead valve engine, although built by Continental, was an exclusive Massey-Harris engine in that Continental did not sell this engine to any other customers, unlike the flathead engines. The 44 was the basis for several other tractor models, including military tractors, export tractors, and industrial tractors. These models are discussed in later chapters. Also, an orchard and vineyard model were built on the 44 standard chassis.

Production Figures:

1946	11
1947	4,147
1948	10,442
1949	16,364
1950	16,955
1951	19,942
1952	12,534
1953	3,360
Total	83,755

Production by Model
(1946–1951)

Gas Standard	18,176
Gas Row-Crop	32,889
Diesel Standard	5,395
Diesel Row-Crop	4,655
Kero Standard	5,821
Kero Row-Crop	3,202
LP Standard and Row-Crop	459
Gas Vineyard	30
Gas Orchard	119
Diesel Orchard	33
Gas High Altitude Row-Crop	268

Massey-Harris Model 44.

Gas High Altitude Standard	64
(1952–1953)	
Not Kept by Model	12,644

Serial Numbers: (Located on plate mounted at rear of left frame member. Also stamped on top left center of transmission housing.)

Model 44 Std (Gas)

1946	1,001–1,140
1947	1,141–1,870
1948	1,871–4,527
1949	4,528–9,580
1950	9,581–13,725
1951	13,726–17,058
1952	17,059–19,117
1952	40,001–43,699
1953	43,700–47,060

Model 44 Row-Crop (Gas)

1946	1,001
1947	1,002–2,047
1948	2,048–5,317
1949	5,318–13,821
1950	13,822–21,814
1951	21,815–31,189

1952	31,190–33,890
1952	40,001–43,699
1953	43,700–47,060

Model 44K Std. (Kerosene)

1946	1,001–1,010
1947	1,011–1,440
1948	1,441–3,597
1949	3,598–4,826
1950	4,827–6,018
1951	6,019–6,786
1952	6,787–6,822
1952	40,001–43,699
1953	43,700–47,060

Model 44K Row-Crop (Kerosene)

1947	1,001–1,078
1948	1,079–1,855
1949	1,856–2,598
1950	2,599–3,328
1951	3,329–4,203
1952	40,001–43,699
1953	43,700–47,060

Model 44D Std. (Diesel)

1948	1,001–1,022
1949	1,023–2,179
1950	2,180–3,988
1951	3,989–5,638
1952	5,639–6,396
1952	40,001–43,699
1953	43,700–47,060

Model 44D Row-Crop (Diesel)

1949	1,001–1,003
1950	1,004–2,482
1951	2,483–4,703
1952	4,704–5,656
1952	40,001–43,699
1953	43,700–47,060

Model 44 Vineyard

1950	1,001–1,030
1951	1,031

(all models)

1952	40,001–43,699

(all models)
1953   43,700–47,060

Model 44 Orchard
1950   1,001–1,100
1951   1,101–1,120

(all models)
1952   40,001–43,699

(all models)
1953   43,700–47,060

Model 44D Orchard
1950   1,001
1951   1,002–1,034

Model 44 Butane (LP) Std.
1952   1,001–1,035

Model 44 Butane (LP) Row-Crop
1952   1,001–1,460

Model 44 GRA (Hi Alt) Row-Crop
1951   1,001–1,163
1952   1,164–1,269

Model 44 GSA (Hi Alt) Std.
1951   1,001–1,054
1952   1,055–1,065

Engine: (Continental Built) Cylinders: four; Bore: 3 7/8; Stroke: 5 1/2; rpm: full load, 1,350; no load, 1,525; Displacement: 260 (cubic inches); Ignition: battery; spark plug Champion "8 Comm"; spark plug gap: .025 inch; Valve clearance intake: .014 inch; Valve clearance exhaust: .014 inch; Electrical system: 6 volt positive ground, Autolite.

Belt Pulley: Diameter: 13 1/2 inches; Face: 6 1/4 inches; Speed: free engine, 975; Belt feet per minute: 3,051 under full load.

Power Takeoff: Spline size: 1 3/8 inches; Speed: 534 rpm.

Transmission Speeds: (miles per hour at 1,350 rpm engine speed) with 12x30 tires.

	Std	RC
1st	2.21	2.48
2nd	3.31	3.75
3rd	4.43	4.98
4th	5.75	6.47
5th	12.28	13.80
Reverse	2.09	3.26

Wheels and Tread: (rubber tires)

	Std	RC	Orchard & Vineyard
Front wheel tire size	6.00x16	5.50x16	6.00x16
Rear wheel tire size	13x30	12x38	13x26

General Dimensions:

	Std	RC	Orchard & Vineyard
Length overall	127 1/8"	135 1/4"	127 1/8"
Width overall	68 9/16"	79"	46"
Height overall	77 1/2"	80"	67 1/4"

Weight:

	Std	RC	Orchard & Vineyard
Front	1,560	1,500	
Rear	2,925	2,665	
Total	4,485	4,165	4753

Turning Radius:

	Std	RC	Orchard & Vineyard
	10' 7"	8' 5 1/2"	11'

Capacities: (Standard) Main fuel tank: 20 gallons; Auxiliary tank (44K): 1 1/2 gallons; Cooling system: 23 quarts; Engine oil pan: 8 quarts; Oil filter: 1 quart; Transmission: 8 gallons.

Capacities: (Row-Crop) Main fuel tank: 25 gallons; Auxiliary tank (44K): 1 1/2 gallons; Cooling system: 23 quarts; Engine oil pan: 8 quarts; Oil filter: 1 quart; Transmission: 9 gallons.

Nebraska Tractor Test: Test No. 389 (Gas) (October 1947)

Serial Number Tested: # 44GR1018

Drawbar horsepower 39.9, belt horsepower 45.6.

Test No. 426 (Diesel Std) (September 1949)

Serial Number Tested: # 44DS1116

Drawbar horsepower 37.9, belt horsepower 43.04.

Test No. 427 (Kerosene Std) (September 1949)

Serial Number Tested: # 44KS4370

Drawbar horsepower 36.8, belt horsepower 39.4.

Retail Prices: (1951)

- 44 Gas Std: $2,387.00
- 44 Gas Row-Crop: $2,316.00
- 44 Kerosene Row-Crop: $2,363.00
- 44 Diesel Row-Crop: $3,094.00

Massey-Harris Model 44 Gas Orchard.

- 44 Orchard Gas: $2,504.00
- 44 Vineyard: $2,445.00

Standard Equipment: Self-starter, velvet ride seat, belt pulley, muffler, flare fenders.

Optional Equipment.
- Crown fenders: Standard only, $17.50
- Hydraulic lift, $168.00
- Lights, $23.50
- Power takeoff, $25.75
- Single front wheel, $199.00
- High arch wide front, $243.00
- Bendix brakes, $31.75
- Long rear axles: 112", $70.00
- Hour meter, $26.75
- 150 lb. rear wheel weight, $16.75
- 80 lb. front wheel weight, $11.50

Color: 1947 Models: Chassis: red; engine: black; wheels: straw yellow. 1948–1953 Models: Chassis: red; engine: red; wheels: straw yellow.

Massey-Harris Model 44-6

In 1947, with the introduction of the new series of Massey-Harris tractors, a six-cylinder tractor remained in the lineup of tractors offered. It was a carryover of the popular 101 Senior tractor and retained the same six-cylinder 226-cubic-inch Continental engine that the 101 Senior used. This engine was also used in the Massey-Harris self-propelled corn picker. The tractor design was updated to match the other tractors in the lineup; in fact, many non-engine 44-4 cylinder parts and 44-6 cylinder parts were the same. However, the larger four-cylinder engine in the 44-4 offered more power and reliability and proved to be more popular with the farmer. In 1951, the 44-6 production ended. The 44-6 was only produced in a gas version.

Production Figures:

1946	1
1947	2,981
1948	2,372
1949	500
1950	383
1951	420
Total	6,657

Serial Numbers:

Model 44-6 Std.

1947	1,001–2,000
1948	2,001–2,600
1950	2,601–2,729

Model 44-6 Row-Crop

1946	1,001
1947	1,002–2,982
1948	2,983–4,754
1949	4,755–5,254
1950	5,255–5,508
1951	5,509–5,928

Engine: (Continental Red Seal) Cylinders: six; Bore: 3 5/16 inches; Stroke: 4 3/8 inches; rpm (drawbar full load): 1,500; rpm (drawbar no load): 1,720 to 1,728; rpm (belt full load): 1,800; rpm (belt no load): 1,975 to 1,985; Displacement: 226 cubic inches; Compression ratio: 6.23 to 1; Firing order: 1,5,3,6,2,4; Pounds of compression cranking speed: 115 to 120 pounds.

Clutch: Foot-operated single plate dry disc.

Belt Pulley: Diameter: 13 1/2 inches; Face: 6 inches.

Massey-Harris Model 44-6.

Power Takeoff: Spline size: 1 3/8 inches; Speed, no load: 632 to 634 rpm at 1,720 to 1,728 engine rpm; Speed, full load: 551 rpm at 1,500 engine rpm; Height from ground: 34 inches.

Foot Brakes: Expanding shoe type, single or dual acting.

Transmission Speeds: Standard (13x30 tires) 1st: 2.46 miles per hour; 2nd: 3.44 miles per hour; 3rd: 4.29 miles per hour; 4th: 6.01 miles per hour; 5th: 12.02 miles per hour. Reverse: 2.78 miles per hour.

Tire Size: Standard: Front: 6.00x16; Rear 13x30.

Tread: Standard: Front: 47 1/2; Rear: 54 1/8.

General Dimensions: Standard: Length: 129 inches; Width: 68 inches; Height: 76 1/2 inches.

Transmission Speeds:

Row-Crop	11x38 Tires	12x38 Tires
1st	2.67	2.76
2nd	3.73	3.85
3rd	4.66	4.81
4th	6.53	6.74
5th	13.06	13.48
Reverse	3.02	3.12

Tire Size: Row-Crop: Front: 5.50x16; Rear 12x38.

Tread: Rear: 52 to 88 inches.

General Dimensions: Row-Crop: Length (overall): 137 inches; Width (over ends of axles): 79 inches; Height (over steering wheel): 82 inches.

Turning Radius: Standard: 11 feet; Row-Crop: 9 feet.

Capacities: (Row-Crop or Standard) Main fuel tank (Row-Crop): 23 gallons, Standard: 19 gallons; Cooling system: 4 gallons; Engine oil pan: 5 quarts; Oil filter: 1 quart; Transmission: 13 gallons; Steering gear housing: 1 quart; Hydraulic tank (Row-Crop): 7 quarts.

Weight: (less fuel, water, etc.) Row-Crop: 3,600 pounds; Standard: 4,200 pounds.

Nebraska Tractor Test: None

Retail Price: (February 1951)
  • 44-6 Row-Crop: $2,178.00

Standard Equipment: Self-starter, velvet ride seat, belt pulley, muffler, fenders.

Options:
  • Hydraulics, $168.00
  • Mechanical power lift, $143.00
  • Single front wheel, $199.00
  • High arch wide front, $243.00
  • Lights, $24.00
  • Bendix brakes, $32.00
  • 112" rear axle, $70.00
  • Hour meter, $27.00
  • 150 lb. rear wheel weight, $17.00
  • 80 lb. front wheel weight, $12.00

Color: 1947 models: Chassis: red; engine: black; wheels: straw yellow. 1948–51 models: Chassis and engine: red; wheels: straw yellow.

Massey-Harris Model 44 Special (SP)

In 1953, the 44 tractor was updated with a larger, 277-cubic-inch engine. The engine had the same block as the earlier 44 260-cubic-inch engine, but had a larger bore to increase the tractor's horsepower. Other newer tractor features offered as options were such extras as live PTO and three-point hitches. The 44 Special was the only Massey-Harris tractor to be offered in a cane or high crop version. Only a few cane tractors were built and most were recalled to the factory, so only a handful of cane tractors exists today. 44 Special distillate, high altitude, and LP tractors had 260-cubic-inch engines.

Production Figures: (All Models)

1953		1,364
1954		6,703
1955		2,652
	Total	10,719

Serial Numbers:

Model 44- Special (G & D)

1953	50,001–51,363
1954	51,364–58,066
1955	58,067–60,719

Massey-Harris Model 44 Special LP Standard Tractor.

Engine: (Continental Built) Model H277; Cylinders: four; Bore: 4 inches; Stroke: 5 1/2 inches; Displacement: 277 cubic inches; Compression ratio: 6.25 to 1; Firing order: 1,3,4,2; Pounds of compression cranking speed: 120 to 130 P.S.I.

Speed: (At crankshaft) Full throttle, no load: 1,520 to 1,530 rpm; Full throttle, full load: 1,350 rpm; Low idle: 480 to 550 rpm.

Clutch: Foot-operated single dry plate.

Belt Pulley: Diameter: 13 1/2 inches; Face: 6 1/2 inches.

Power Takeoff: Spline size: 1 3/8 inches; Speed: Full throttle, no load: 601 to 605 rpm, full throttle, full load: 534 rpm.

Transmission Speeds: (miles per hour)

		Row-Crop-Standard			
Rubber Tires	11-38	12-38	13-38	13-30	14-30
1st	2.40	2.46	2.54	2.19	2.27
2nd	3.62	3.72	3.84	3.31	3.42
3rd	4.82	4.95	5.11	4.40	4.55
4th	6.25	6.44	6.64	5.72	5.92
5th	13.38	13.77	14.20	12.28	12.65
Reverse	3.16	3.25	3.35	2.86	2.96

Wheel and Tread (Rubber Tires):

Row-Crop   Standard Front Tire Size
      6.50-16 (Tricycle)
      7.50-16
      9.00-10 (Single Front)

Rear Tire Size
      Standard   11-38/12-38/13-28
      Row-Crop   13-30 or 14-30

Length
      Standard   140 inches
      Row-Crop   137 inches

Width
      Standard   73 1/2 inches
      Row-Crop   68 1/2 inches

Height (over steering wheel):
      Standard   78 3/4 inches
      Row-Crop   82 1/8 inches

Weight: less fuel and operator
      Gas Standard, 14x30 tires   5,325 pounds
      Gas Row-Crop, 13x38 tires   5,283 pounds

Turning Radius:
      Standard   12 1/2 feet
      Row-Crop   9 feet

Massey-Harris Model 44D Special.

Capacities: Main fuel tank: 23 gallons; Cooling system: 22 quarts; Engine oil: 7 quarts; Transmission case: 13 gallons; Steering housing: 1 quart.

Distillate and High Altitude Gasoline

Engine: (Continental) Model H260; Cylinders: four; Bore: 3 7/8 inches; Stroke: 5 1/2 inches; Displacement: 260 cubic inches; Compression ratio: Distillate 4.68 to 1, High altitude gas 6.65 to 1; Firing order: 1,3,4,2; Pounds compression cranking speed: Distillate, 80 to 85 pounds; High altitude gas, 125 to 135 pounds.

Liquified Petroleum

Engine: (Continental) Model H260; Cylinders: four; Bore: 3 7/8 inches; Stroke 5 1/2 inches; Displacement: 260 cubic inches; Compression ratio 8.7 to 1; Firing order: 1,3,4,2; Pounds compression cranking speed: 180 to 190 pounds.

Diesel, Including Cane Tractor

Engine: (Continental) Model H260; Cylinders: four; Bore: 3 7/8 inches; Stroke: 5 1/2 inches;

Cane tractor wheels: Drive wheels: 13x38; Front wheels: 7.50x18; Wheelbase: 99 13/16 inches.

Cane tractor speeds: 1st: 2.54 miles per hour; 2nd: 3.84 miles per hour; 3rd: 5.11 miles per hour; 4th: 6.64 miles per hour; 5th: 14.20 miles per hour. Reverse: 3.35 miles per hour.

Cane Tractor Weight: 6,456 pounds.

Nebraska Tractor Test: Test No. 510 (October 1953)

Serial Number Tested: #44G15F 50001

Drawbar horsepower 43.58; belt horsepower 48.95.

Retail Prices: (1955)

 44 Special Gas Row-Crop: $2,681.00

 44 Special Diesel Row-Crop: $3,415.00

 44 Special LP Row-Crop: $2,882.00

 44 Special Standard: $2,689.00

 44 Special Cane Diesel: $4,536.00

Standard Equipment: Self-starter, velvet ride seat, fenders, muffler, lights, hour meters on diesels.

Options:

- Live PTO, $136.00
- 114" rear axle, $34.00
- 3-point hitch, $150.00
- Lift shaft, $50.00
- Hydraulics, $226.00
- Belt pulley, $20.00
- Power takeoff, $29.00
- Cigarette lighter, $3.00
- Single front wheel, $223.00
- High arch wide front, $201.00
- 100 lb. front wheel weight, $16.00
- 180 lb. frame weights, $34.00
- Ether injection for diesels, $21.00
- Block heater for diesels, $5.00
- Hour meter, $30.00

Color: Frame and engine: red; wheels: straw yellow.

Massey-Harris Model 33 (G, K, and D)

The Model 33 was introduced in late 1952 to replace the Model 30 in the Massey-Harris tractor lineup. The diesel version of the Model 33 was produced in limited quantities. Although no actual production figures exist by engine type, some former Massey employees report that only 150 diesel versions were made.

Production Figures: (All Models)

Late 1952	1,054
1953	4,562
1954	3,165
1955	2,826
Total	11,607

Serial Numbers: (All Models)

1952	1,001–2,054
1953	2,055–6,616
1954	6,617–9,781
1955	9,782–12,607

Engine: (Continental Built) Model E201 (gas and diesel); Cylinders: 4; Bore: 3 5/8 inches; Stroke: 4 7/8 inches; Displacement: 201 cubic inches; Compression ratio: 5.95 to 1 (gas), 15 to 1 (diesel); Firing order: 1,3,4,2; Pounds compression cranking speed: 110 to 120 PSI.

Massey-Harris Model 33K Standard Tractor.

Massey-Harris Model 33 Diesel.

Speed: (at crankshaft) Full throttle, no load: 1,660-1,685 rpm; Full throttle, full load: 1,500 rpm.

Clutch: Foot-operated single dry plate.

Belt Pulley: Diameter: 13 1/2 inches; Face: 8 1/2 inches; Speed: Full throttle, no load: 985 to 1,000 rpm.

Power Takeoff: Spline size: 1 3/8 inches; Speed: Full throttle, no load: 610 to 619 rpm, Full throttle, full load: 551 rpm.

Foot Brakes: Single or dual acting.

Transmission Speeds: (miles per hour)

	Row-Crop-Standard		
Rubber Tires	11-38	12-38	12-28
1st	2.67	2.75	2.27
2nd	3.73	3.84	3.17
3rd	4.66	4.80	3.96
4th	6.53	6.72	5.55
5th	13.08	13.46	11.11
Reverse	3.03	3.11	2.57

Wheels and Tread: (Rubber Tires)

Row-Crop	Standard	
Front Tire Size	5.50x16	5.50x16
Front tread	8-35/64-60-1/4	47-19/32

Rear Tire Size   11x38 or 12x38   12x28

General Dimensions:

	Row-Crop	Standard
Length	127 inches	125 inches
Width	69 inches	64 1/16 inches

Height (over steering wheel) 79 inches 73 inches

Weight: 3,820 pounds.

Turning Radius: Row-Crop: 9 feet; Standard: 11 feet.

Capacities: Main fuel tank: 19 gallons; Cooling system: 4 1/2 gallons; Engine oil: 7 quarts; Transmission case: 13 gallons (Row-Crop), 12 gallons (Standard); Steering housing: 1 quart; Filter: 1 quart; Hydraulic system: 14 quarts (Row-Crop), 13 quarts (Standard).

Injection Pump (Diesel): Bosch single plunger.

Nebraska Tractor Test: Test No. 509 (October 1953)

Serial Number Tested: # 33GIRF4960

Drawbar horsepower 35.5; belt horsepower 39.5.

Retail Prices: (1955)

   33 Gas Row-Crop: $2,095.00

   33 Diesel Row-Crop: $2,770.00

   33 Gas Standard: $2,135.00

   33 Diesel Standard: $2,810.00

Regular Equipment: Rubber tires, self-starter, lights, battery, ammeter, thermostat, oil gauge, oil filter, air cleaner, internal PTO shaft, drawbar, seat, fenders, toolbox.

Options:

   • Independent PTO, $136.00
   • Hydraulic lift, $176.00
   • Cast center rear wheels, $92.00
   • 112" long rear axle, $16.00
   • Three-point Hitch-all, $150.00
   • Belt pulley, $19.00
   • External PTO, $29.00
   • Lights, $26.00
   • High arch front axle, $201.00
   • Single front wheel, $223.00
   • Hour meter, $30.00
   • 80 lb. front wheel weights, $13.00
   • 150 lb. rear wheel weight, $19.00

Color: Chassis and engine: red; wheels: straw yellow; starter, generator and radiator: black.

Massey-Harris Model 55 (G, K, D, and LP)

The Model 55 was introduced in 1947 as the replacement for the 201, 202, 203 series of tractors. It was advertised as being the world's most powerful tractor with its new 382-cubic-inch engine in 1947 ads. The 55 was a popular tractor in the western plains of the United States and western Canada.

Production Figures: (All Models)

1947	1,293
1948	2,627
1949	3,235
1950	2,968
1951	2,999
1952	3,454
1953	2,390
1954	1,787
1955	1,038
1956	140
Total	21,931

Serial Numbers: (starting serial number each year)

Model 55 Gas-Standard

1946	1,001
1947	1,116
1948	2,132
1949	3,581
1950	5,468
1951	6,399–7,077
1952	10,001
1953	13,017
1954	15,299
1955	17,059–17,888

Model 55D

Riceland & Hillside

1950	1,001
1951	1,152
1952	1,452–1,516
1952	10,001
1953	13,017
1954	15,299
1955	17,059–17,888

Massey-Harris Model 55 cane Tractor.

Model 55 High Altitude
(GSA, GSWA, GSHA)
1951	1,001
1952 (GSWA)	1,025–1,026
1952	10,001
1953	13,017
1954	15,299

Model 55K-Standard
1946	1,001
1947	1,013
1948	1,554
1949	3,033
1950	4,078
1951	4,808
1952	5,503–5,504
1952	10,001
1953	13,017
1954	15,299
1955	17,059–17,888

Model 55
(Gas Western)(GSW)

Year	Serial
1951	1,002
1952	1,083–1,109
1952	10,001
1953	13,017
1954	15,299

Model 55D-Standard

Year	Serial
1949	1,001
1950	1,022
1951	2,058
1952	2,822–2,964
1952	10,001
1953	13,017
1954	15,299
1955	17,059–17,888

Model 55 DISH
(Diesel Western)(DSW)

Year	Serial
1951	1,001
1952	1,190–1,212
1952	10,001
1953	13,017
1954	15,299

Model 55G
(Riceland & Hillside)

Year	Serial
1949	1,001
1950	1,035
1951	1,216–1,509
1952	10,001
1953	13,017
1954	15,299
1955	17,059–17,888

Model 55K
(Riceland & Hillside)

Year	Serial
1949	1,001
1950	1,013
1951	1,110–1,230
1952	10,001
1953	13,017
1954	15,299
1955	17,059–17,888

Massey-Harris Model 55 Diesel.

Engine: (Continental Built) Cylinders: four; Bore: 4 1/2 inches; Stroke: 6 inches; rpm, full load: 1,350, no load: 1,510 to 1,520; Displacement: 382 cubic inches; Overhead valve type.

Pounds Compression, Cranking Speed: Gasoline: 100 minimum, 105 maximum; Low-grade models: 70 minimum, 75 maximum; Compression ratio (gasoline) 5.65 to 1; Compression ratio (low-grade fuel) 4.65 to 1; Compression ratio (diesel) 15 to 1.

Clutch: Foot-operated, single-plate dry disc. Hand operated (optional).

Belt Pulley: Diameter: 16 inches; Face: 8 inches; Speed, no load: 817 to 822; Speed engine rpm 1,350; full load 730.

Power Takeoff: Spline size: 1 3/8 inches, 6B; Speed, no load: 583 to 587 rpm; Speed, full load: 521 rpm.

Foot Brakes: Expanding shoes. Individual action, or pedals interlocked.

Transmission Speeds: (15x34 tires) 1st: 3.08 miles per hour; 2nd: 4.39 miles per hour; 3rd: 5.42 miles per hour; 4th: 12.53 miles per hour. Reverse: 2.64 miles per hour.

Wheels and Tread: Front wheels 7.50x18, tread 52 3/16 inches; Rear wheels 14x34, tread 57 5/16 inches; Rear wheels 15x34, tread 57 5/16 inches.

General Dimensions: Length overall: 145 inches; Width overall: 72 1/2 inches; Height overall: 83 1/4 inches.

Weight: Shipping weight (gas): 6,920 pounds; Shipping weight (low grade): 7,048 pounds.

Turning Radius: 12 feet.

Capacities: Main fuel tank: 27 1/2 gallons; Auxiliary tank (55K): 1 1/2 gallons; Cooling system: 7 gallons; Engine oil pan (including filter): 2 1/2 gallons; Transmission and master gear housing: 17 gallons; Belt pulley: 1 quart; Hydraulic system (extra equipment): 3 1/2 gallons.

Injection Pump (diesel): Bosch (PSB or APE)

Nebraska Tractor Test: Test No. 452 (Diesel) (October 1950)

Serial Number Tested: # 55DS1827

Drawbar horsepower 54; belt horsepower 60.

Test No. 455 (Gas) (April 1951)

Serial Number Tested: # 55GS6184

Drawbar horsepower: 60.

Belt horsepower: 68.

Retail Prices: (1951)

        55 Gas: $3,214.00

        55 Diesel: $4,142.00

        55 Gas Riceland: $3,482.00

        55 Diesel Riceland: $4,410.00

        55 Butane (LP): $3,577.00

Regular Equipment: Rubber tires, self-starter, battery, thermostat, oil gauge, water temperature indicator, internal PTO shaft; air cleaner, oil filter, ammeter, voltage regulator, drawbar.

Options:

- Lights, $24.00
- Crown fenders, $76.00
- 150 lb. rear wheel weight, $17.00
- Power takeoff, $27.00
- Hand clutch instead of foot clutch, $40.00

Color: 1947 Models: Radiator and engine: black; chassis and frame: red; wheels: straw yellow. 1948–1955 Models: Engine, chassis, and frame: red; wheels: straw yellow; radiator: black.

Massey-Harris Pony (Model 11)

The Pony was introduced in 1947 and was a very popular tractor in vegetable farms and gardens. Worldwide, more Pony tractors were produced than any other Massey tractor (Models 11, 812, 14, and 820). Producing 12 horsepower, the Pony had several mounted implements designed just for this tractor, including a plow, cultivator, front blade, sickle mower, planter, disk, loader, and others. Ponys are popular with collectors today, due to their small size and ease of storage and transport. All Model 12 Ponys were built in Woodstock, Ontario, Canada. In 1954–55, some Ponys were painted gray and distributed through Ferguson dealers.

Production Figures:

1947	1,314
1948	9,073
1949	5,106
1950	2,834
1951	4,543
1952	4,087
1953	962
1954	705
1957	122
Total	28,746

Serial Numbers: (starting serial number each year)

	Adjustable Front Axle (PGA)	Standard Front Axle (PGS)
1947	1,001–1,002	1,001–1,320
1948	1,003–3,514	1,321–4,162
	1,001A–1,570A	—
1949	1,571A–10,816A	—
1950	10,817A–13,725A	4,163–4,328
1951	13,726–18,224	—
1952	18,225–22,006	—
1953	22,007–22,668	—
1954	22,669–23,853	—
1957	24,049–24,319	—
Gray Pony		
1954	23,149–23,853	
1955	24,090	

Engine: Heavy-duty industrial, L-head type-; Cylinders: four; Compression ratio: 6.5 to 1; Displacement: 62 cubic inches; Bore: 2 3/8 inches; Stroke 3 1/2 inches. (Continental Built)

Massey-Harris Pony Tractor.

Engine Speed: Drawbar: 1,800 rpm; Belt: 1,990 rpm.

Pistons: Aluminum Alloy, Anodized.

Cooling System: 13-inch fan, 7-quart capacity.

Carburetor: Schebler.

Tank Capacity: 7 gallons.

Manifold: Intake and exhaust are one piece cast integral.

Air Cleaner: Oil flush type.

Lubrication: Full pressure; Capacity: 3.3 quarts; Pump, oil filter, transmission: oil bath: 3 quarts; Rear axle: oil bath; Chassis: high pressure grease.

Governor: Built-in centrifugal.

Ignition: Self-starter, regular: battery, Auto spark. 6-volt system positive ground.

Speeds: At 1,800 rpm: 1st: 2.74 miles per hour; 2nd: 3.59 miles per hour; 3rd: 7.00 miles per hour. Reverse: 3.2 miles per hour.

Clutch: Borg & Beck, single-plate foot-operated, 6 1/2 inches.

Drive Wheels: (rubber only) 8-24, 9-24, or 6-30.

Front Wheels: 4.00x15.

Wheelbase: 66 inches.

Tread: 41 inches to 75 1/2 inches.

Brakes: Individual rear wheel can be locked.

Belt Pulley: Diameter: 6 inches; Face: 5 1/2 inches; Speed 1,990 at 1,800.

Depth-O-Matic or Mechanical Lift: Optional.

Weight: 1,365 pounds.

Nebraska Tractor Test: Test No. 401 (September 1948)

Serial Number Tested: # PGS3461

Drawbar horsepower 11; belt horsepower 12.

Retail Prices: (1951)

Pony: adjustable front axle: $854.00

Pony: standard front axle: $838.00

Standard Equipment: Rubber tires, self-starter, muffler, fenders, draw-bar.

Options:

- Belt pulley and PTO, $59.00
- Hand lift, $66.00
- Hydraulic lift, $79.00
- ASAE drawbar, $7.00
- Lights, $20.00
- Pair of front wheel weights 50 lb. each, $9.00
- Pair of rear wheel weights 100 lb. each, $21.00

Color: 1947 Models: Engine: black; chassis: red; wheels: straw yellow. 1948–1957 Models: Engine and chassis: red; wheels: straw yellow. Ferguson Pony 1954–1955: All gray.

Massey-Harris Pony (Model 14)

The Model 14 Pony was an industrial version of the Model 11 Pony. All items are the same as the Model 11 Pony except for the clutch, which operated with a hydraulic coupling for heavy hauling jobs such as towing aircraft, barges, or rail cars. Production was very limited. It was produced only with the adjustable front axle.

Production Figures:

1951	33
1952	17
1953	24
Total	74

Serial Numbers: (Unavailable)

Specifications: Same as No. 11 Pony, except clutch with hydraulic coupling.

Weight: 1,896 pounds.

Price: (1953)

Model 14 Pony: $1,073.00

Color: Chassis & engine: red; wheels: straw yellow.

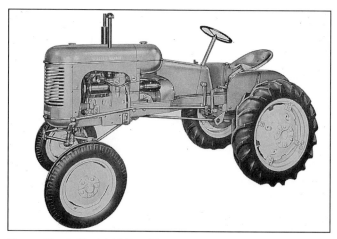

Massey-Harris Model 14 Pony Tractor.

Massey-Harris 811, 812, and 820 Pony

The 811 and 812 Pony tractors were built in France from 1951 to 1957. The 820 Pony replaced the 812 Pony, and was built from 1957 through 1961. These Pony tractors were based on the same chassis as the North American Pony but were fitted with Simca and Hanomag engines. The tractors were sold in Europe. In 1963, the Massey Ferguson Model 25 or 825 in Europe replaced the Pony tractor.

Production Figures:

Model:	811	812	820	821
1951	1,813	—	—	—
1952	10	5,800	—	—
1953	—	8,133	—	—
1954	—	8,758	—	—
1955	—	11,536	—	—
1956	—	13,101	—	—
1957	—	1,894	11,953	—
1958	—	—	14,297	—
1959	—	—	4,033	4,036
1960	—	—	948	5,004
1961	—	—	46	355
Total	1,823	49,222	31,277	9,395

Serial Numbers: (Unavailable)

Model 812

Regular Equipment: Tires, self-starter, battery, instrument panel group, fenders, telescoping front axle, drawbar, set of wheel weights for rear wheels.

Rating: One-Plow, 25 to 30 cm. Maximum horsepower 15.

Engine: Four-cylinder, 4-stroke, overhead valve. Bore 72 mm. Stroke 75 mm. Displacement 1.221 cubic cm. Compression ratio 6.2 to 1. (Simca Built).

Engine Speed: Governed, 1,000 to 1,800 rpm.

Governor: Centrifugal type.

Ignition: 6-volt battery.

Carburetor: Downdraft.

Fuel: Regular gasoline.

Fuel Tank Capacity: 28 liters (5 1/2 Imperial gallons)

Lubrication: Combination pressure and splash. Full pressure to bearings.

Cooling System: Thermo syphon. Radiator capacity: 7 liters. Full-length water jacketing.

Massey-Harris 812 Pony Tractor.

Speeds: At 180 rpm. First, 4 km. 400; Second, 5 km. 780; Third, 11 km. 270; Reverse, 5 km. 180.

Transmission: Spur gear-type with heavy drop gear drive to main axle. Ball and roller bearings.

Clutch: Single dry disc.

Belt Pulley: Diameter, 152 mm.; Width, 133 mm.; Speed, 1,990 rpm; Belt speed 953 meters per minute.

Power Takeoff: Diameter, 28 mm. 57 (1 1/8 inches); Speed, 540 rpm.

Tires: Rear 8.00x24; Front 4.00x15.

Wheelbase: 1 m. 67.

Front Tread Adjustment: 1 m.04 to 1 m.75.

Rear Tread Adjustment: 1 m.04 to 1 m.75.

Turning Radius: 2 m.59.

Minimum Weight: With lift attachment, less operator, 800 kgs; with rear wheel weights and liquid ballast in tires, 1.080 kgs.

Special Equipment: Hand lift attachment, front tool bar for implements, drive combined with pulley, lights, extra wheel weights for rear, weights for front wheels, 9.00x24 tires.

Model 820 Diesel

Engine: Type: Diesel D621-E54 (Hanomag); number of cylinders: two (vertical); Cycle: two stroke; Power: 18 B.H.P.; Injection: air turbulence chamber; Bore: 85 mm; Stroke: 90 mm; Cubic capacity: 1021 cc.; Compression ratio: 18 to 1; Maximum engine speed: 1930 rpm; Engine speed under load: 1800 rpm; Slow running speed: 450 rpm; Speed governor: centrifugal with flexible coupling; Cylinders: wet, removable; Cylinder heads: removable, water cooled.

Lubrication: Lubricating system: pressure oil lubrication.

Fuel Injection System: Injection pump: Bosch type PF 2 K 55. Injection spill timing: 27 degrees before T.D.C.; Fuel lift pump: Bosch type FP/KS 22 F8 single action; Air filter: oil bath type.

Cooling System: Double water circuit with water pump and thermostat.

Electrical Equipment: Battery: 12 volts; Pre-hearing plugs: Bosch, 0.9 volts, assembled in series.

Retail Prices: Unavailable.

Color: Chassis and engine: red; wheels: straw yellow.

Massey-Harris Pacer (Model 16)

The Pacer was introduced in 1954 as a larger, improved model of the North American Pony. In appearance, it looks a lot like the Pony, but has a larger, 91-cubic-inch engine, a padded seat, and hydraulic lift as standard equipment. The frame is slightly longer than a Pony frame.

Production Figures:

1953	164
1954	1,444
1955	1,159
Total	2,767

Serial Numbers:

1954	50,001–51,612
1955	51,613–52,770
1956	52,771–53,730

Engine: Four-cylinder industrial, L-head, 91-cubic-inch displacement; 2 7/8-inch bore, 3 1/2-inch stroke, 6.1 to 1 compression ratio. Continental Built.

Engine Speed: Governed rpm 1,000 to 1,800, full load.

Cooling System: 13-inch fan, 9-quart capacity, 4-pound pressure radiator cap.

Fuel: Gasoline.

Carburetor: Marvel-Schebler.

Fuel Tank Capacity: 7 1/2 gallons.

Air Cleaner: Oil bath.

Lubrication: Crankcase capacity 3 1/2 quarts (dipstick marking including 1 pint for oil filter). Transmission capacity: 3 1/2 quarts; Rear axles capacity 1 3/4 quarts for each drop housing; Spur gear oil pump and removable cartridge oil filter.

Ignition: 6-volt battery, automatic spark control.

Speeds: At 1,800 rpm with 9-24 tires: 1st: 2.88 miles per hour; 2nd: 3.77 miles per hour; 3rd: 7.35 miles per hour. Reverse: 3.37 miles per hour. At 1,800 rpm with 10-24 tires: 1st: 3.02 miles per hour; 2nd: 3.98 miles per hour; 3rd: 7.7 miles per hour. Reverse: 3.57 miles per hour.

Clutch: Single-plate foot-operated, 6 1/2 inch.

Steering: Cam and lever, irreversible.

Drive Wheels: Rubber tires only, 9-24, 10-24, or 6-30.

Front Wheels: Rubber tires only, 4.00x15.

Wheelbase: 72 1/4 inches.

Tread: Rear, with 9-24 tires, adjustable from 41 inches to 69 inches.

Massey-Harris Pacer Tractor.

With 10-24 tires, adjustable from 45 inches to 69 inches. With 6-30 tires, adjustable from 38 inches to 71 inches. Reversible rear wheels. Front tread, with standard axle, adjustable from 44 inches to 68 inches in 4-inch steps. Maximum front tread, by reversing front wheels, 75 1/2 inches. Narrow front axle available, giving adjustment from 38 inches to 58 inches.

Brakes: Individual rear wheel with pedal lock for simultaneous operation.

Belt Pulley: (optional equipment) Diameter: 6 inches; Face: 5 1/4 inches; Speed 1,990 rpm at 1,800 rpm.

Power Takeoff: (optional equipment) 540 rpm at 1,800 rpm engine speed.

Depth-O-Matic Hydraulic System.

Lights: Two headlights, one rear, with connecting cables.

Nebraska Tractor Test: Test No. 531 (November 1954)

Serial Number Tested: # PGA 50891

Drawbar horsepower 17; belt horsepower 19.

Retail Price: (1955)

Pacer: $1,369.00

Regular Equipment: Battery ignition, self-starter, oil gauge, heat gauge, ammeter, independent and dual rear brakes, padded seat, toolb.ox, muffler, adjustable front axle, drawbar, air cleaner, gas filter, oil filter, rubber tires, hydraulic lift.

Massey-Harris Pacer (Model 16)

Options Equipment:
- Belt pulley and PTO, $68.00
- Market Garden wheels & tires 6x30, $108.00
- 2 50 lb. front wheel weights, $10.00
- 2 100 lb. rear wheel weights, $22.00

Color: Chassis and engine: red; wheels: straw yellow; radiator and shroud: black.

Massey-Harris Colt (Model 21)

The Colt and Mustang tractors replaced the Model 22 Massey-Harris. The Colt and Mustang were essentially the same tractor except for engine size. Exhaust was directed downward on the Colt and Mustang tractors, and three-point hitches, even though optional equipment, are commonly found on these tractors.

Production Figures:

1952	416
1953	1,253
Total	1,669

Serial Numbers:

1952	1,001–1,416
1953	1,417–2,669

Engine: Heavy-duty industrial, L-head, type; Cylinders: four; Compression ratio: 6.47 to 1; Displacement: 124 cubic inches; Bore: 3 inches; Stroke: 4 3/8 inches. Continental Built.

Engine Speed: Drawbar: 1,500 rpm; Belt: 1,800 rpm.

Cooling System: Tubular radiator, with bypass thermostat. Centrifugal, ball bearing packless sealed pump. Full-length water jackets. 16-inch fan. 12-quart capacity.

Massey-Harris Colt Tractor.

Fuel: Gasoline.

Carburetor: Schebler 7/8 inch adjustable

Tank Capacity: 13 gallons.

Manifold: Intake and exhaust are one piece cast integral.

Air Cleaner: Oil bath.

Lubrication: Full pressure. Capacity: 5 quarts; Pump: spur gear; Oil filter: removable cartridge; Transmission: oil bath; Rear axle: oil bath; Chassis: high pressure grease.

Ignition: 6-volt system.

Speeds: At 1,500 rpm: 1st: 2.45 miles per hour; 2nd: 3.51 miles per hour; 3rd: 4.61 miles per hour; 4th: 12.99 miles per hour. Reverse: 2.45 miles per hour.

Clutch: Single-plate foot-operated, 9 inch.

Drive Wheels: (rubber only) Row-Crop: 10-28; Standard 10-28.

Front Wheels: High Arch: 4.00x15; Row-Crop: 4.00x15; Standard: 5.00x15. Single front wheel: 6.00x12.

Wheelbase: High Arch: 87 inches; Row-Crop: 82 3/4 inches; Standard: 76 inches; Single front wheel: 82 3/4 inches.

Tread: High Arch (adjustable) 52 to 88 inches; Standard: 52 inches.

Brakes: Individual rear wheel.

Belt Pulley: Regular, diameter: 9 1/2 inches; Face: 6 inches; Speed: 1,224 at 1,800.

Power Takeoff: (extra equipment) (PTO rpm at maximum engine rpm) 551 at 1,500. Two-Way Follow-Up Hydraulic System.

Weight: 2,566 pounds.

Nebraska Tractor Test: None.

Retail Prices: (1955)

    Colt - Standard: $1,340.00
    Colt - Row-Crop - Tricycle: $1,465.00
    Colt - Row-Crop - Adjustable Wide Front: $1,505.00
    Colt - Row-Crop - Single Front: $1,486.00

Regular Equipment: Rubber tires, self-starter, battery, thermostat, oil gauge, internal PTO shaft, air cleaner, oil filter, ammeter, hitch bracket, adjustable tread, seat, fenders.

Options:

  • Three-point hitch, $45.00
  • Velvet ride seat, $29.00
  • Hour meter, $30.00
  • Belt pulley, $41.00

- Power takeoff, $27.00
- Lights, $23.00
- Pair of 90 lb. front frame weights, $31.00
- Grille screen, $3.00
- 150 lb. rear wheel weight, $19.00

Color: Chassis and frame: red; wheels: straw yellow; radiator and shroud: black.

Massey-Harris Mustang Model 23

The Mustang replaced the Model 22. Improvements included a downward exhaust, three-point hitch options, and front step for mounting tractor toward front of operator platform.

Production Figures:

1952	257
1953	3,088
1954	207
1955	220
1956	60
Total	3,832

Serial Numbers:

1952	1,001–1,665
1953	1,666–4,345
1954	4,346–4,552
1955	4,553–4,772
1956	4,773–4,832

Engine: Heavy-duty industrial, L-head type; Cylinders: four; Compression ratio: 6.50 to 1; Displacement: 140 cubic inches; Bore: 3 3/16 inches; Stroke: 4 3/8 inches. Continental Built.

Engine Speed: Drawbar: 1,500 rpm; Belt: 1,800 rpm.

Cooling System: 16-inch fan; 12-quart capacity.

Fuel: Gasoline.

Carburetor: Schebler 7/8 inch adjustable

Tank Capacity: 13 gallons.

Lubrication: Full pressure. Capacity: 5 quarts; Pump: spur gear; Oil filter: removable cartridge; Transmission: oil bath; Rear axle: oil bath; Chassis: high pressure grease.

Ignition: 6-volt system.

Transmission: All gears carburized and hardened.

Speeds: At 1,500 rpm: 1st: 2.55 miles per hour; 2nd: 3.66 miles per hour; 3rd: 4.81 miles per hour; 4th: 13.54 miles per hour. Reverse: 2.55 miles per hour.

Clutch: Single-plate foot-operated, 9 inch.

Drive Wheels: (rubber only) Row-Crop 11-28, 12-28; Standard 11-28.

Front Wheels: Row-Crop: 4.00x15; Standard: 5.00x15, Single front wheel: 6.00x12.

Wheelbase: High Arch: 87 inches; Row-Crop: 82 3/4 inches; Standard: 75 3/4 inches; Single front wheel: 82 1/2 inches.

Tread: Row-Crop (adjustable): 52–88 inches; Standard: 52 inches.

Massey-Harris Mustang Tractor.

Belt Pulley: Regular, diameter: 9 1/2 inches; Face: 6 inches; Speed: 1,224 at 1,800; Feet per minute: 3,044. Power Takeoff: (Extra Equipment) (PTO rpm at maximum engine rpm) 551 at 1,500.

Two Way Follow-Up Hydraulic System

Distillate Models: Fundamentally the same as gasoline models (hot manifold). Mustang "K"; Compression ratio: 5 to 1; Cubic inch displacement: 140 inches.

Weight: 2,785 pounds.

Nebraska Tractor Test: None.

Retail Prices: (1955)

Mustang - Standard: $1,466.00

Mustang - Adjustable Wide Front Gas Row-Crop: $1,655.00

Mustang - Tricycle Row-Crop - Gas: $1,616.00

Mustang - Single Front Row-Crop - Gas: $1,635.00

Mustang - Distillate Tricycle Row-Crop: $1,646.00

Regular Equipment: Rubber tires, self-starter, battery, thermostat, oil gauge, internal PTO shaft, air cleaner, oil filter, ammeter, drawbar bracket, adjustable tread, seat fenders.

Options: (same as Colt tractor)

Color: Chassis and engine: red; wheels: straw yellow; radiator and shroud: black.

Massey-Harris Model 333 (G, K, D, and LP)

The 333 tractor replaced the Model 33 in 1956. It carried a new paint scheme, chrome grille trim and a dual-range transmission, giving the operator 10 speeds forward and 2 in reverse.

Production Figures:

1956	2,648
1957	100
Total	2,748

Serial Numbers:

1956	20,001–22,648
1957	22,649–22,748

Engine: Continental Model E208; Cylinders: four; Bore: 3 11/16 inches; Stroke: 4 7/8 inches; Displacement: 208 cubic inches; Compression ratio: 6.5 to 1; Firing order: 1,3,4,2; Pounds compression cranking speed: 125 to 135 P.S.I. Speed: (at crankshaft) Full throttle, no load: 1,670 to 1,685 rpm; Full throttle, full load: 1,500 rpm.

Clutch: Foot-operated single dry plate.

Belt Pulley: (optional equipment) Diameter: 13 1/2 inches; Face: 6 1/2 inches; Speed: full throttle, full load: 876 rpm.

Power Takeoff: Spline size, 1 3/8 inches; Speed: Full throttle, full load: 543 rpm.

Wheels and Tread: (rubber tires)

Front Tire Size

Row-Crop	5.50-16	
Standard	5.50-16	

Rear Tire Size

Row-Crop	11-38	12-28
Standard	12-38	13-28

General Dimensions: (Row-Crop) Length: 140 1/2 inches; Width: 76 inches; Height (over steering wheel): 75 inches. Weight: (Gas Row-Crop with 12x38 tires): 5,654 pounds.

Turning Radius: 14 feet.

Capacities: Main fuel tank: 23 gallons; Cooling system: 17 1/2 quarts; Engine oil: 7 quarts; Transmission case: 13 gallons; Steering housing: 1 quart; Filter: 1 quart; Hydraulic system: Row-Crop 12 quarts, Standard 11 quarts; Add 1 quart when equipped with power steering.

Injection Pump: (Diesel) Type: PSB - Single Plunger; Speed - Crankshaft Speed; Timing: Pump: Port Closing, Flywheel: 22 degrees BTDC.

Nebraska Tractor Test: Test No. 577 (Diesel) (June 1956)

Massey-Harris
Model 333
Tractor.

Serial Number Tested: # 20,848
Drawbar horsepower 35; belt horsepower 39.
Test No. 603 (Gas) (October 1956)
Serial Number Tested: # 22,173
Drawbar horsepower 39; belt horsepower 44.
Retail Prices: (1957)
    333 Standard - Diesel: $2,963.00
    333 Standard - Gas: $2,413.00
    333 Row-Crop - Diesel: $2,872.00
    333 Row-Crop - Gas: $2,322.00
Regular Equipment: Lights, 12-volt electrical system, velvet ride seat,
    10-speed transmission, muffler, PTO, tractor meter, fenders.
Options:
    • Live PTO, $136.00
    • Hydraulic lift, $280.00
    • Power steering, $135.00
    • Single front wheel, $33.00
    • High arch, adjustable wide front, $106.00
    • Cast center rear wheels, $92.00
Color: Engine: bronze; chassis and hood: red; wheel centers: straw
yellow; rear wheel rims: aluminum; fan and shroud: black; grille
screen: straw yellow.

Massey-Harris Model 444 (G, K, D, and LP)

The 444 tractor replaced the Model 44 Special in 1956. It carried a new paint scheme, chrome grille trim, and a dual-range transmission with 10 speeds forward and 2 in reverse.

Production Figures:

1956	3,989
1957	3,143
1958	261
Total	7,393

Serial Numbers

1956	70,001
1957	73,989–77,131
1958	77,132–77,393

Engine: (Continental Built) Model H277; Cylinders: four; Bore: 4 inches; Stroke: 5 1/2 inches; Displacement: 277 cubic inches; Compression ratio: 6.25 to 1; Firing order: 1,3,4,2; Pounds compression cranking speed: 130 to 140 P.S.I. Speed: (at crankshaft) Full throttle, no load: 1,670 to 1,685 rpm; Full throttle, full load: 1,500 rpm.

Clutch: Foot-operated single dry plate.

Belt Pulley: Diameter: 13 1/2 inches; Face: 6 1/2 inches; Speed: full throttle, no load: 1,122 to 1,132 rpm, full throttle, full load: 1,008 rpm.

Power Takeoff: Spline size, 1 3/8 inches; Speed: full throttle, full load: 543 rpm.

Wheels and Tread: (rubber tires)

	Row-Crop	Standard
Front Tire Size	6.50-16	7.50-16
Rear Tire Size	11-38/12-38/13-38	13-30 or 14-30

General Dimensions: Length: 150 1/4 inches; Width: 76 inches; Height (over steering wheel): 76 3/4 inches.

Weight: 5,258 pounds.

Capacities: Main fuel tank: 23 gallons; Cooling system: 22 quarts; Engine oil: 7 quarts; Transmission case: 13 gallons; Steering housing: 1 quart; Filter: 1 quart; Hydraulic system: 12 quarts.

Injection Pump: (Diesel) Type - PSB - Single Plunger; Speed - Crankshaft Speed; Timing: Pump: Port Closing, Flywheel: 25 degrees BTDC.

Nebraska Tractor Test: Test No. 576 (Diesel) (June 1956)

Serial Number Tested: # 71,402

Drawbar horsepower 46, belt horsepower 51.

Test No. 602 (LP) (October 1956)

Serial Number Tested: # 72,917

Massey-Harris Model 444 Tractor.

Drawbar horsepower 47; belt horsepower 52.
Retail Prices: (1957)
       444 Gas Row-Crop Tricycle: $2,919.00
       444 Diesel Row-Crop Tricycle: $3,619.00
       444 Gas Standard: $2,979.00
       444 Diesel Standard: $3,679.00
Standard Equipment: Lights, 12-volt system, velvet ride seat, fenders, 10-speed transmission, power adjust rear wheels, muffler, PTO, tractor meter.
Options:
- Live PTO, $136.00
- Hydraulic lift, $350.00
- Power steering, $135.00
- Three-point hitch, $100.00
- Single front wheel, $223.00
- Belt pulley, $60.00
- Cigarette lighter, $3.00
- 100 lb. front wheel weight, $16.00
- 150 lb. rear wheel weight, $19.00
- Rear safety light, $12.00
Color: Engine: bronze; chassis and hood: red; wheel center: straw yellow; rear wheel rims: aluminum; radiator and shroud: black.

Massey-Harris Model 555 (G, K, D, and LP)

The 555 Massey-Harris replaced the 55 tractor in the lineup in 1956. Few changes were made from the 55. The color scheme and chrome were updated to match the 333 and 444 tractors. The engine and transmission are the same as the Model 55.

Production Figures:

1955	132
1956	1,000
1957	1,880
1958	782
Total	3,794

Serial Numbers:

1955	20,001–20,132
1956	20,133–21,132
1957	21,133–23,012
1958	23,013–23,794

Engine: (Continental Built) Model J382; Cylinders: four; Bore: 4 1/2 inches; Stroke: 6 inches; Displacement: 382 cubic inches; Compression ratio (gasoline) 5.65 to 1, (distillate) 4.65 to 1; Firing order: 1,3,4,2; Pounds compression cranking speed (gasoline) 100 to 105 P.S.I., (distillate) 70 to 75 P.S.I.

Ignition: Battery; Electrical system: 12 volt.

Speed: (at crankshaft) Full throttle, no load: 1,510 to 1,520 rpm; Full throttle, full load: 1,350 rpm.

Clutch: Foot- or hand-operated, single dry plate.

Belt Pulley: Diameter: 16 inches; Face: 8 inches; Speed: Full throttle, no load: 822 to 826 rpm; Full throttle, full load: 730 rpm.

Power Takeoff: Spline size, 1 3/8 inches, 6B; Speed full load: 521 rpm.

Foot Brakes: Expanding shoes. Individual action, or pedals interlocked.

Transmission Speeds: (Standard Models)

	14x34 Tires	15x34 Tires
1st	2.96 mph	3.08 mph
2nd	4.22 mph	4.39 mph
3rd	5.22 mph	5.42 mph
4th	12.07 mph	12.53 mph
Reverse	2.54 mph	2.64 mph

Wheels and Tread:

Massey-Harris Model 555 Tractor.

Front wheels 7.50x18   Tread 52 3/16 inches
Rear wheels 14x34   Tread 57 5/16 inches
Rear wheels 15x34   Tread 57 5/16 inches

General Dimensions: Length overall: 145 9/16 inches; Width overall:
72 1/2 inches; Height overall: 83 1/4 inches.

Weight: Gas: 6,920 pounds; Low grade: 7,048 pounds.

Turning Radius: 12 feet.

Transmission Speeds: 18x26 tires

	Western Special	Riceland
1st	2.82 mph	3.02 mph
2nd	4.01 mph	4.31 mph
3rd	4.95 mph	5.32 mph
4th	11.45 mph	12.30 mph
Reverse	2.41 mph	2.59 mph

General Dimensions:

	Western Special Rubber	Riceland Special Rubber
Wheelbase	89 inches	89 inches
Tread, Front	57 3/4 inches	57 3/4 inches
Tread, Rear	70 inches	70 inches
Width	89 1/4 inches	91 3/8 inches
Height	64 7/8 inches	65 3/4 inches

Tires:

	Western Special Rubber	Riceland Special Rubber
Rear	18x26	18x26
Front	7.50x18	7.50x18
	Three rib	Single rib

Weight: Riceland Special with water, fuel and oil, rubber tires: 6,624 pounds. Western Special: approx. 6,500 pounds.

Capacities: Main fuel tank: 27 1/2 gallons; Auxiliary tank (55K) 1 1/2 gallons; Cooling system (55G) 7 gallons, (55K) 7 1/4 gallons; Engine oil pan, including filter: 2 1/2 gallons; Transmission and master gear housing: 1 quart; Hydraulic system (extra equipment): 3 gallons; Power steering supply tank: 2 1/2 quarts.

Nebraska Tractor Test: None

Retail Prices: (1956)

     555 Gas: $3,736.00

     555 Diesel: $4,511.00

     555 LP : $3,986.00

     555 Riceland Gas: $4,204.00

     555 Riceland Diesel: $4,979.00

     555 Western Special Gas: $4,119.00

     555 Western Special Diesel: $4,894.00

Standard Equipment: Velvet ride seat, crown fenders, hour meter, lights, muffler, foot clutch, 12-volt system.

Options:

- Hand clutch, $42.00
- Power steering, $161.00
- Belt pulley, $71.00
- Power takeoff, $31.00
- Cigarette lighter, $3.00
- Hydraulics, $202.00

Color: Engine: bronze; chassis and hood: red; wheel centers: straw yellow; rear wheel rims: aluminum; radiator and shroud: black.

Massey-Harris Model 50

The Massey-Harris Model 50 is the result of the 1953 merger of the Massey-Harris and Ferguson companies. In 1955, Ferguson introduced the Ferguson 40 tractor. Massey-Harris dealers were offered the same tractor as a Model 50. The Ferguson 40 and Massey-Harris 50 are the same tractor, except for the sheet metal. In 1958, Ferguson and Massey-Harris dealers were brought together and the tractor became the Massey-Ferguson Model 50.

Production Figures:

1955	472
1956	10,291
1957	4,944
Total	15,707

Serial Numbers:

1955	500,001–500,472
1956	500,473–510,763
1957	510,764–515,707

Engine: (Continental Z134) Cylinders: four; Bore: 3 5/16 inches; Stroke: 3 7/8 inches; Displacement: 134 cubic inches; Compression ratio: 6.6 to 1; Firing order: 1,3,4,2; Pounds compression cranking speed: 145 P.S.I.

Speed: (at crankshaft) Full throttle, no load: 2,175 to 2,225 rpm; Full throttle, full load: 2,000 rpm.

Belt Pulley: (optional) Diameter: 9 inches; Face: 6 1/2 inches.

Power Takeoff: Constant running with proportional ground speed, or standard. Spline size, 1 3/8 inches.

Wheels and Tread: (rubber tires)

	Tricycle	Utility
Front Tire Size	550-16	550-16
Rear Tire Size	10-38	11-28
Front tread width	49-81	48-80
Rear tread width	48-76	48-76

Wheel Torque Wrench Tension: Rear wheel to axle: 80–90 feet pounds; Front wheel: 65–75 feet pounds.

General Dimensions:

	Tricycle	Utility
Wheelbase	81.18 inches	81.18 inches
Width	58 inches	51 inches
Height (over steering wheel)	62 5/8 inches	58 3/4 inches

Weight: (less fuel & operator) 3,000 pounds.

Massey-Harris Model 50 Tractor.

Capacities: Fuel tank: 17 gallons; Cooling system: 10 quarts; Engine: 5 quarts; Oil filter: 1 quart; Transmission: 8 gallons; Steering housing: 2 pints.
Nebraska Tractor Test: Test No. 595 (September 1956)
Serial Number Tested No. 509603
Drawbar horsepower 32; belt horsepower 34
Retail Prices: (1957)

MH 50 Utility:	$2,352.00
MH 50 High Arch:	$2,461.00
MH 50 Tricycle Front:	$2,402.00

Standard equipment: Three-point hitch, dual clutch, six-speed transmission, two reverse, 12-volt system, tractor meter, deluxe seat, live PTO, ground drive PTO.
Options:
- Power steering, $120.00
- Belt pulley, $15.00
- Lights, $30.00
- Vertical exhaust, $4.00

Color: Engine and chassis: bronze; hood and fenders: red; wheel centers: red; rear rims: aluminum.

Massey-Harris Model 303 (Work Bull)

In an effort to get into the industrial market for tractors, Massey-Harris-Ferguson developed a 303 industrial tractor from the 333 standard agricultural tractor. The industrial tractors were named Work Bulls. The 303 and 404 Work Bulls were eventually dropped for the Ferguson design of tractors, so production was limited. Early 303 tractors had 333 sheet metal. Sheet metal was changed in 1958 to provide a heavier frame and chassis.

Production Figures:

1956	75
1958	118
1959	794
Total	987

Serial Numbers:

Old Style Sheet Metal	1956	1,001–1,075
Old Style Sheet Metal	1957	1,076–1,193
Old Style Sheet Metal	1958	1,194–1,377
New Style Sheet Metal	1958	1,378–1,987

Engine: Continental Model E208; Cylinders: four; Bore: 3 11/16 inches; Stroke: 4 7/8 inches; Displacement: 208 cubic inches; Compression ratio: 6.5 to 1; Firing order: 1,3,4,2; Pounds compression cranking speed: 125 to 135 P.S.I.

Speed: (at crankshaft) Full throttle, no load: 1,670 to 1,685 rpm; Full throttle, full load: 1,500 rpm.

Clutch: 11-inch foot-operated single dry plate.

Power Takeoff: Spline size, 1 3/8 inches; Speed: full throttle, full load: 543 rpm.

Wheels and Tread:

Front Tread	Front Tire	Rear Tread	Rear Tire
54-3/8	7.50x18 6 ply	58 or 66	14x30 6 ply
54-5/8	7.50x15 10 ply	64-1/4	13x24 8 ply
54-5/8	7.50x15 12 ply	64-1/4	14x24 8 ply

General Dimensions:

Wheelbase: 85 1/2 inches

Length 7.50x15 and 13x24 tires: 133 inches

7.50x18 and 14x30 tires: 134 1/2 inches

Width Rear Max. 13x24 - 78 3/4 inches

13x30 - 81 1/4 inches

Massey-Harris Model 303 Work Bull Tractor.

Height over steering wheel
7.50x18 and 14x30 tires - 76 1/4 inches
7.50x15 and 13x24 tires - 73 3/4 inches
Weight: 13x24 tires: 5,260 pounds.
Turning Radius: Manual steering: 13 1/2 feet; Power steering 14 3/4 feet.
Capacities: Main fuel tank: 23 gallons; Cooling system: 23 quarts; Engine oil (including filter): 8 quarts; Transmission case: 13 gallons; Steering gear: 1 quart; Power steering: 2 1/2 quarts.
Nebraska Tractor Test: None.
Retail Prices: Unavailable.
Color: Chassis, engine, and wheels: industrial yellow; rear wheel rims: aluminum.

Massey-Harris Model 404 (Work Bull)

The 404 Work Bull was the industrial version of the 444 Standard tractor. Unable to sell the 404 and 303 as industrial tractors, the company eventually sold some in Kansas as standard tread farm tractors by Massey.

Production Figures:

1956	50
1957	68
Total	118

Serial Numbers:

1956	1,001–1,050
1957	1,051–1,118

Engine: Continental Model H277; Cylinders: four; Bore: 4 inches; Stroke: 5 1/2 inches; Displacement: 277 cubic inches; Compression ratio: 6.25 to 1; Firing Order: 1,3,4,2; Pounds compression cranking speed: 130 to 140 P.S.I.

Speed: (at crankshaft) Full throttle, full load: 1,500 rpm.

Clutch: Foot-operated 12-inch single dry plate.

Power Takeoff: Spline size, 1 3/8 inches; Speed: full throttle, full load: 543 rpm.

Foot Brakes: Expanding show: individual action or pedals interlocked.

Wheels and Tread:

Front Tread	Front Tire	Rear Tread	Rear Tire
54 3/8	7.50x18 6 ply	58 or 66	14x30 6 ply
54 5/8	7.50x15 10 ply	64 1/4	14x24 8 ply
54 5/8	7.50x15 12 ply	64 1/4	14x24 8 ply

General Dimensions:

Length 7.50x15 and 14x24 tires: 133 inches

7.50x18 and 14x30 tires: 134 1/2 inches

Width 14x24 tires: 79 1/2 inches

14x30 tires: 74 1/4 inches

Height over steering wheel

7.50x18 and 14x30 tires: 77 inches

7.50x18 and 14x24 tires: 74 1/4 inches

Weight: 5,420 pounds.

Turning Radius: Manual steering: 13 1/2 feet; Power steering: 14 3/4 feet.

Capacities: Main fuel tank: 23 gallons; Cooling system: 22 quarts; Engine oil: 7 quarts; Transmission case: 13 gallons; Filter: 1 quart; Power steering: 2 1/2 quarts.

Massey-Harris Model 404 Work Bull Tractor.

Nebraska Tractor Test: None.

Retail Prices: Unavailable.

Color: Chassis, hood, engine, and wheels: industrial yellow; rear wheel rims: aluminum.

Massey-Harris I-162 Military Tractor

Massey-Harris contracted with the Army in 1953 to build 26 tractors for use on air bases as tow tractors and utility tractors.

Production Figures:
    1953   26
Serial Numbers:
    1953   1,001–1,026
Engine: Continental 162 cubic inch (refer to MH 30 tractor for the same engine specifications).
Weight: 5,675 pounds.
Drawbar Pull: 3,000 to 3,700 pounds.
Maximum Speed: 13 miles per hour.
Tire Size: Front: 6.00x16; Rear 12x28.
Nebraska Tractor Test: None.
Retail Price: Military contract.
Color: Entire tractor: Army green.

Massey-Harris Model I-162 Military Tractor.

Massey-Harris I-244 Tractor

The I-244 was built under military contracts for both the Navy and the Air Force. These tractors were used on aircraft carriers and on airfields, and had magnetic sweeps installed to pick up debris on the runways. These tractors were built under three separate military contracts.

Production Figures:

1955	237
1956	224
1957	247
Total	708

Serial Numbers: (No PTO)

1955	1,001–1,019	Navy
1956	1,020–1,038	Navy
1956	3,001–3,180	Air Force
1957	3,181–3,427	Air Force

Model FSI-244 with PTO

1955	2,001–2,218	Air Force
1956	2,219–2,243	Air Force

Engine: Continental Model I-244; Cylinders: six; Bore: 3 7/16 inches; Stroke: 4 3/8 inches; Displacement: 244 cubic inches; Compression ratio: 6.9 to 1; Firing order: 1,5,3,6,2,4; Pounds compression cranking speed: 130 to 142 pounds at 170 rpm.

Electrical System: 6 volt.

Ignition: Magneto.

Speed: (at crankshaft) Full throttle, no load: 1,650 to 1,655 rpm; Full throttle, full load: 1,500 rpm.

Clutch: Foot-operated single dry plate.

Power Takeoff: Spline size, 1 3/8 inches; Speed: Full throttle, full load: 551 rpm.

Foot Brakes: Single or dual acting.

Transmission Speed: Rubber tires, 14x28 tire. 1st: 2.45 miles per hour; 2nd: 3.44 miles per hour; 3rd: 4.29 miles per hour; 4th: 6.00 miles per hour; 5th: 12.02 miles per hour. Reverse: 2.69 miles per hour.

Wheels and Tread: (Rubber tires) Front Tire Size: 7.50x16 6-ply rib-type puncture proof; Front tread width center to center: 52 1/8 inches; Rear Tire Size: 14x28 8 ply-Road Builder; Front tire pressure: 36 pounds; Rear tire pressure: 25 pounds; Rear tread: 58 3/4 inches.

General Dimensions: Length: 136 5/8 inches; Width: 73 1/8 inches;

Massey-Harris Model I-244 Tractor.

Height (over steering wheel): 72 1/2 inches; Height (over air cleaner stack): 76 1/4 inches.

Weight: 6,480 pounds.

Turning Radius: 12 feet 6 inches.

Capacities: Main fuel tank: 23 gallons; Cooling system: 3 3/4 gallons; Engine oil: 1 1/4 gallons; Transmission and master gear housing: 12 gallons; Filter: 1 quart.

Nebraska Tractor Test: None.

Retail Price: Military contract.

Color: Probably industrial yellow, entire tractor.

Massey-Harris Model I-330-G

Six tractors were built for the Navy in 1954 with a 330-cubic-inch Continental engine. This is perhaps one of the rarest of all Massey tractors of the 1950s.

Production Figures:
1954: 6
Serial Numbers:
1954   1,001–1,006
Engine: 330-cubic-inch Continental (See 203 Massey-Harris for details of this engine).
Nebraska Tractor Test: None.
Retail Price: Military contract.
Color: Unknown.

Massey-Harris 744 (England)

The Massey-Harris 744 was built in England from 1948 through 1953. It used the North American–based Massey-Harris 44 chassis but was fitted with a Perkins Diesel engine. The tractor was offered in a half-track model, as well as standard and Row-Crop rubber tire models.

Production Figures:

1948	16
1949	1,054
1950	2,783
1951	4,660
1952	5,547
1953	2,546
Total	16,606

Serial Numbers:

1948	201– 400
1949	401–1,400
1950	1,401–4,400

After 1950, production year is indicated by a letter: F = 1951; G = 1952, etc.

Engine: Six-cylinder diesel, 42 b.h.p.; 3 1/2 inch bore; 5-inch stroke; 288.6-cubic-inch displacement.

Electrical Equipment: 12-volt heavy-duty battery. Starter motor.

Tank Capacity: 16 gallons.

Belt Pulley: 13 1/2-inch diameter x 6-inch face. 863 rpm.

Power Takeoff Unit: S.A.E. spline 1 3/8-inch diameter, 534 rpm.

Drawbar: Swinging type with 30-inch lateral adjustment.

Drawbar Horsepower: 36.

Wheels and Tire Equipment:

	Standard	Row-Crop
Front Rubber	6.00x19 inches	5.50x16 inches
Rear Rubber	13x30 inches or	12.00x38 inches
		14x30 inches

Transmission Speeds:

	Standard 13x30 Tires	Row-Crop 14x30 Tires	Half-Track Model 12x38 Tires	
High	12.28	12.84	13.80	11.25
Fourth	5.75	6.02	6.47	5.28
Third	4.43	4.64	4.98	4.07
Second	3.33	3.49	3.75	3.06
Low	2.21	2.31	2.48	2.03
Reverse	2.90	3.04	3.26	2.66

Massey-Harris Model 744 Tractor.

Nebraska Tractor Test: None.

Retail Prices: Unavailable.

Color: Hood, chassis, and frame: red; engine: black; wheels: straw yellow.

Massey-Harris Model 745 and 745S (England)

The Model 745 replaced the 744 in 1954 in England. It was fitted with a larger, four-cylinder Perkins engine.

Production Figures:

1954	2,952
1955	2,965
1956	3,126
1957	1,245
1958	889
Total	11,177

Serial Numbers: Unavailable.

Engine: Four-cylinder Perkins L.4 diesel, with replaceable wet cylinder liners; Bore: 4 1/4 inches; Stroke: 4 3/4 inches; Compression ratio: 18.3 to 1; Capacity: 270 cubic inches; Belt horsepower: 45.3; Maximum sustained pull: 6,200 pounds (Standard Model).

Fuel System: Three-stage filtration with circulation by lift pump. Fuel pump fitted with pneumatic governor.

Clutch: Borg & Beck 12AS clutch with Borglite cushion plate; 16 springs; Carbon thrust release bearing.

Transmission: Straight spur gears; five forward speeds, one reverse; speed reduction in three stages only

Power Takeoff: (supplied as extra) 1 3/8 inches S.A.E. spline, 534 rpm at 1,350 rpm engine speed.

Belt Pulley: (supplied as extra) 13 1/2 inches diameter; 6-inch face; 863 rpm at 1,350 rpm engine speed.

Wheel Equipment and Adjustments: Front Wheels: Standard 6.00x19 (cast), General Purpose 6.00x19 (variable track), High-Arch Row-Crop 5.50x16, Twin-Wheel Row-Crop 5.50x16. Rear Wheels: Standard 13x30, 14x30, General Purpose 13x30, 14x30, 11x36, 12x38, High-Arch Row-Crop 12x38, Twin-Wheel Row-Crop 12x38.

Road Speeds: miles per hour at 1,500 rpm

Tire Size   11x36

	13x30	14x30	12x38
1st	2.46	2.57	2.75
2nd	3.70	3.83	4.17
3rd	4.93	5.15	5.54
4th	6.38	6.69	7.19
5th	13.63	14.26	15.33
Reverse	3.22	3.34	3.62

Massey-Harris Model 745 Tractor.

Batteries: Two 6 volt.
Weights: Standard Model: 5,200 pounds; High-Arch Model: 5,100 pounds; Twin-Wheel Model: 4,700 pounds.
General Dimensions:
Approx. Width
Overall Length Overall Height (Adjustable)

	Overall Length	Overall Height	(Adjustable)
High-Arch	147 in.	82 1/4 in.	67–97 in.
Row-Crop Twin	135 in.	82 1/4 in.	67–97 in.
General Purpose	130 3/4 in.	79 7/8 to 82 3/4 in.	67–97 in.
Standard	130 3/4 in.	79 7/8 to 80 1/2 in.	68–69 in.

Capacities: Fuel: 20 gallons; Oil: 2 gallons; Radiator: 4 1/2 gallons.
Extra Equipment: Rear wheel weights; front weight to fit in frame; field lights; PTO shaft; belt pulley; velvet ride seat; hour meter; hydraulic lift and three-point linkage; remote control hydraulic equipment.
Nebraska Tractor Test: None.
Retail Prices: Unavailable.
Color: Engine, chassis, and frame: red; wheels: straw yellow.

Appendix A:

Serial Number Locations and Prefixes

Wallis Tractors: Serial number plate on front of boiler plate frame to right side of hand crank.

Challenger and Pacemaker: Serial number stamped on nameplate left side of frame, also stamped on frame above nameplate.

Model 25: Serial number stamped on nameplate on front end of frame. Also stamped on frame below the nameplate.

Models 81, 101, 201, 202, 203, 20, 22, 30, 33, 44, 55, Colt, Mustang: Serial numbers are stamped on a plate on left side of main frame and are also stamped on the top center of the transmission housing.

On Models 20, 20K, 22, 22K, 30, 30K, 44, 44K, 44B, 44D, 44(6), 55, 55K, 55B, and 55D, the coded suffix letters of serial number are explained below:

A - High altitude engine	K - Low-grade fuel
B - Butane (LP) fuel	O - Orchard
D - Diesel fuel	R - Row-Crop
F - Foot clutch	S - Standard
G - Gasoline	V - Vineyard
H - Hand clutch	W - Wide axle

A 1 or 5 after the G on Massey tractors 1952–1957 means: 1 - Regular altitude; 5 - Hi-altitude.

Pony and Pacer: Tractor serial number is located on plate on right side of front frame, above front axle. Engine serial number is located on left side of cylinder block.

333, 444, and 555 Tractors: Tractor serial number located on right side of frame under gas tank.

Model 50: Serial number located on nameplate on dash.

Note: Engine serial numbers were never tracked by Massey production and are not of any use in dating a tractor. Chassis serial numbers are the numbers used for dating.

Appendix B

Paint Colors

It is getting harder to match old paint numbers to newer paint codes and colors due to changes in lead-based paints, etc. Following is a list of several paint numbers and formulas as we have them. Take them to your paint dealer and hopefully you can find a cross-match.

333, 444, 555 Bronze
NAPA - Martin-Senour Paint
M-H Engine Paint Color
No. 99-23062 00(L) Aztec Gold Met.
(S Single State Acrylic Enamel)
Voc: 4.48 lb.s.

** SS **	NO LEAD	MSDS: ACR-LF PHOTO **
9800	White	3.2 9824
9854	Black	11.5
9844	Trans-Red	16.6
9858	H S Gold	28.1
9836	Clear	71.7
9835	Mix Drier	22.5

NAPA - Acrylic Enamel (Martin Senour)
MH Red - use Ford Regoon Red

Late MH Yellow	99L-4341
MH 25 CH & PA Green	99L-11513
MH 333 & 444 Bronze	99L-5420
Ferguson Gray	99L-3740
MF Flint Gray	99L-3746
MF Red	99L-3823

Sherwin Williams

MH Red	JK-4036R
MH Yellow	JK-4649

Dupont

MH Red-Centari Enamel	674 DH

MH 333 & 444 Bronze-

Centari Enamel (69 GMSaddle Metallic)	5054A

MH & MF Yellow-Dulux

Enamel	29440
MH Red-Dulux Enamel	4294AH

Paint Colors

Ditzler

  MH Red-Acrylic   DQE70364

  MH Yellow   DQE70837

333 & 444 Bronze: A close color is 1973 Mazda Automobile Bronze or 1969 GM Truck Saddle Metallic. (See above for a good NAPA match.)

Wallis Gray:

Ditzler Wallis Gray

DAR 32465 short 499 2-qt. formula

plus 3000 490

plus 200 440

plus 800 482

plus 50 400

plus 40 495

Rustoleum Charcoal Gray: 1 gallon to 1 pint black also approximates the Wallis Gray

Ferguson 35 & 40 Beige: Sherwin Williams

1 gallon B54W101 Industrial Enamel (White)

Add Gold 3 1/4 oz.

Maroon 1/32 oz.

Umber 1 1/16 oz.

White 2 oz.

Appendix C

Other References

Clubs

Friends of Ferguson Heritage. This is a club for those interested in the wide range of tractors and machines developed from the ideas of the late Harry Ferguson, including such derivatives as Ferguson Brown, Ford Ferguson, Massey-Ferguson, Massey-Harris, etc. The club produces three quality magazines a year and organizes events and meetings. Further details from The Secretary, FOFH, P.O. Box 62, Banner Lane, Coventry CV4 9GF, United Kingdom. 1999 subscription rate for overseas members is 17 pounds sterling per year. (If you send a VISA number, they can charge your credit card for the approximate $30 fee.)

Massey Collector's Association. This is a Midwest-based club for collectors of Massey tractors and equipment. Annual membership cost is $20.00. The club sends a bimonthly four-page newsletter to all members. Send membership to: Rita Simmons, Treasurer, Massey Collectors Assn., 2355 County Road 4030, Holts Summit, MO 65043.

Twin Power Heritage Association. Inc. This is an Ontario, Canada-based club for Massey collectors. Annual membership fee is $25.00. Members receive a bimonthly eight-page newsletter. The club meets on a bimonthly basis in Ontario. Membership can be obtained by sending $25.00 to Beverly Hughes, RR No. 3, Ilderton, Ontario, Canada N0M 2A0.

Ferguson Club. The Ferguson Club specializes in Ferguson tractors and equipment and can be contacted via The Secretary, 21 Graytown Avenue, Upper Malone Road, Belfast, BT9 6UG, Northern Ireland, U.K.

Magazine

Wild Harvest - Massey Collector's News is a bimonthly magazine for collectors of Wallis, Massey-Harris, Ferguson, and Massey-Ferguson tractors and equipment. Contents include classified ads for parts and tractors, current events and shows featuring Massey equipment, reprints of old Massey product information, and articles on Massey history and Massey restoration projects. Annual subscription rate is $24.00 in the United States and $28.00 in Canada. Send to Massey Collector's News, P.O. Box 529, Denver, IA 50622.

Books

Condie, Alan T. *Massey Ferguson 1958–1982*. A.T. Condie Publications, 1995

Cook, Peter. *Massey at the Brink*. Collins, 1981

Denison, Merril. *Harvest Triumphant*. The Falcon Press Ltd., 1949

Farnworth, John. *Ferguson Implements and Accessories*. Farming Press, 1996

Farnworth, John. *The Massey Legacy Volume One*. Farming Press, 1997

Farnworth, John. *The Massey Legacy Volume Two*. Farming Press, 1998

Harry Ferguson and I. *Massey Ferguson Tractors Ltd.*, 1993

King, Alan C. *Massey-Harris, An Advertising History*. Independent Print Shop Co., 1988

King, Alan C. *Massey-Harris Data Book No. 6*. Independent Print Shop Co., 1992

Neufield, E.P. *A Global Corporation*. University of Toronto Press, 1969

Wendell, C.H. *Massey Tractors*. MBI Publishing Company, 1992

Williams, Michael. *Massey-Ferguson Tractors*. Farming Press, 1987

Index